MANDALAS AND MORE
(NOT FOR THE FAINT OF HEART)

CREATED BY D J PARRY

ISBN-13: 978-1523235810
ISBN-10: 1523235810

DEDICATION

To all the adults out there who still have a kid inside of them who loves to color.

Special thanks to my friend Jenny Searcy for all her help.

PREFACE

Who didn't like to color when they were a kid? No one that I can remember. And exactly when did we quit coloring? Hmmm....I can't remember that, either. But for some unknown reason, most of us have gone years without coloring. WHAT WERE WE THINKING!!!

No need to worry about it now...coloring is back and bigger than ever FOR ADULTS. It's touted as a way of reducing anxiety and stress, just as it did when we were kids...taking our minds off our troubles, allowing us to unwind.

Of course, coloring for adults is a little more complicated than it used to be. The designs are more challenging and intended to keep your attention for quite a while. Today we have many choices of coloring instruments, including markers, gel pens, sharpies, and lots of different types of colored pencils to choose from. A lot of the designs I have created will require a fine-pointed instrument because the spaces are small and meant to be challenging.

So, grab your coloring instrument of choice and regain some of that childhood bliss we loved so much. It's not gone, after all.

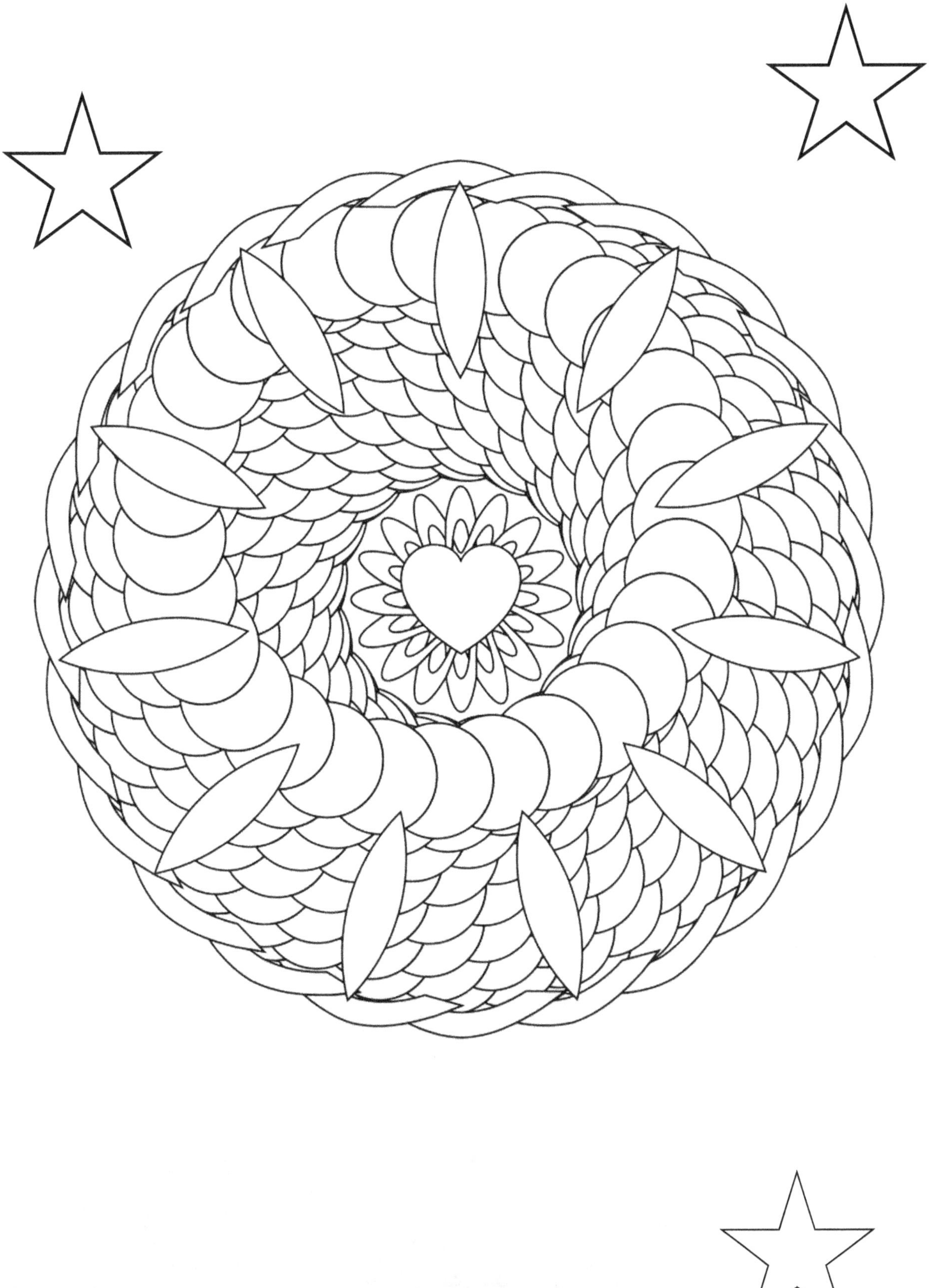

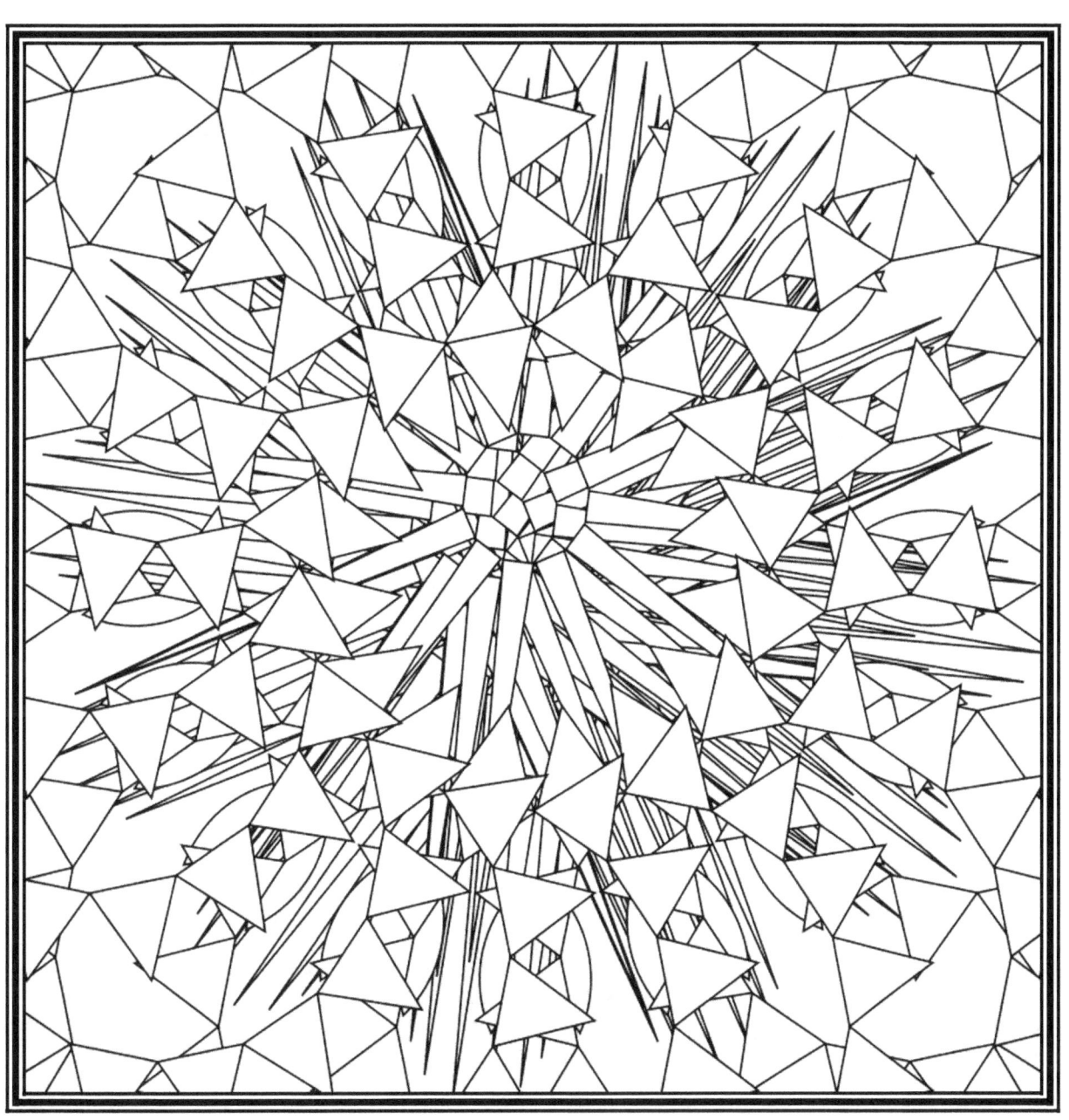

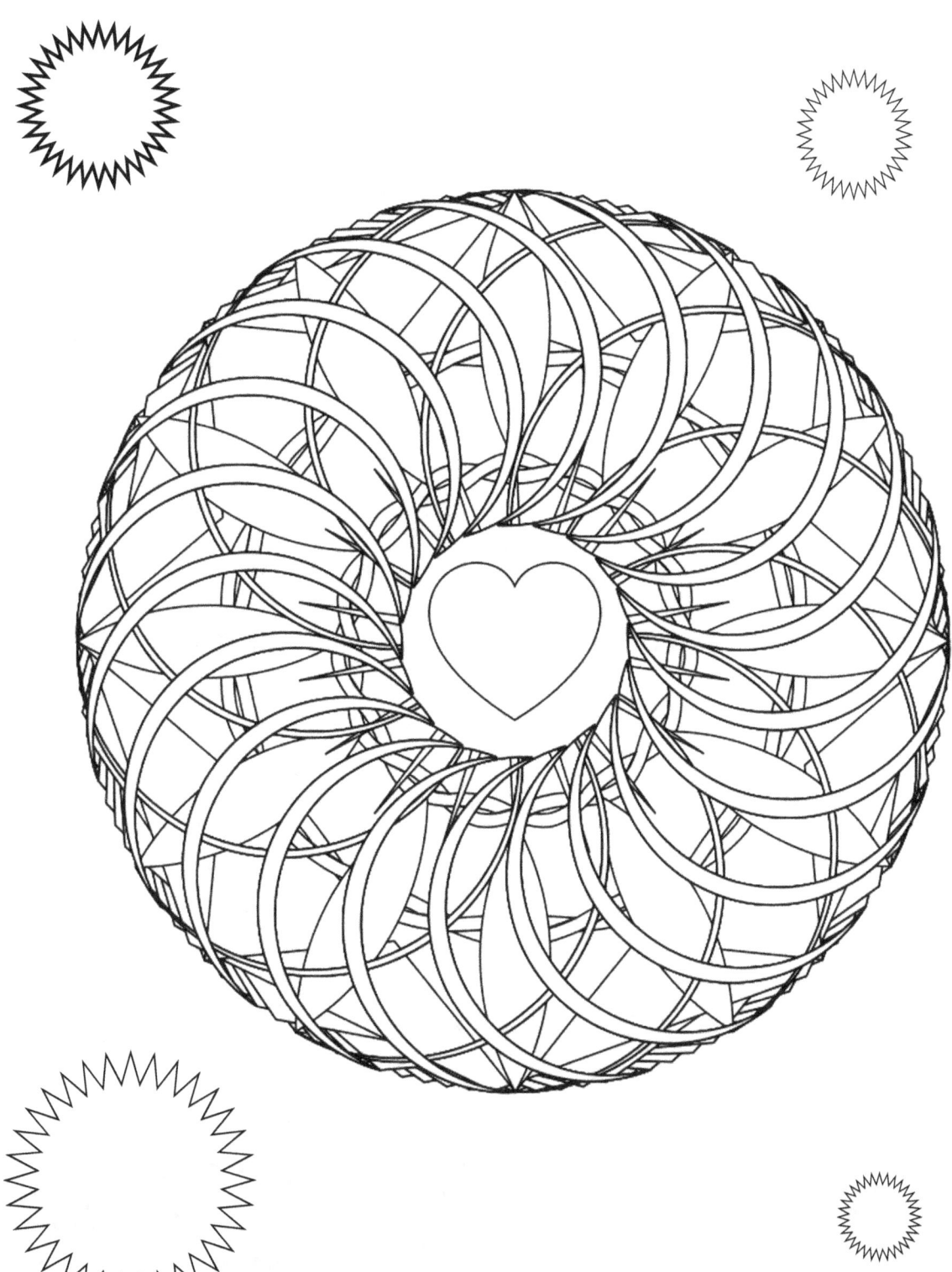

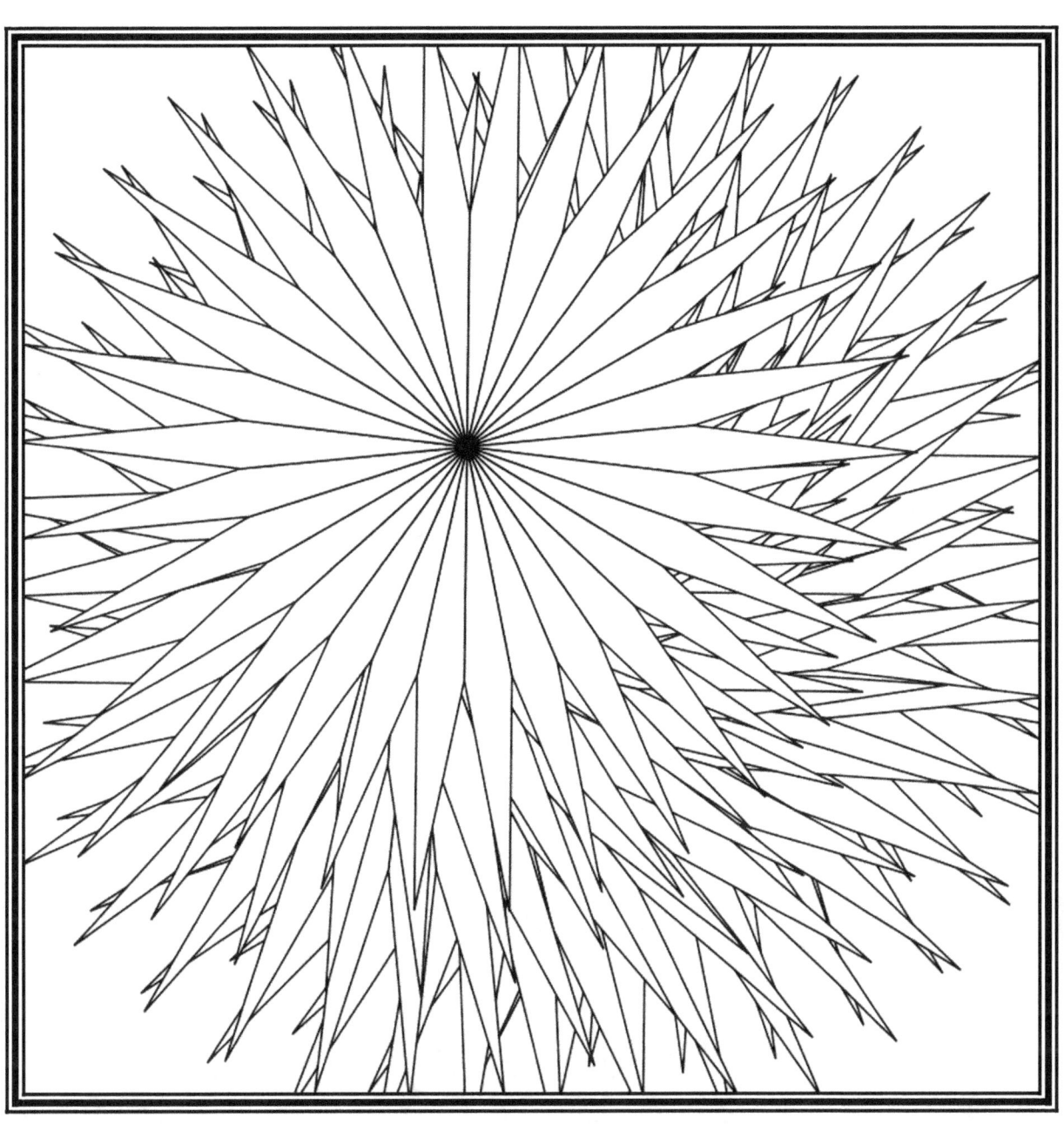

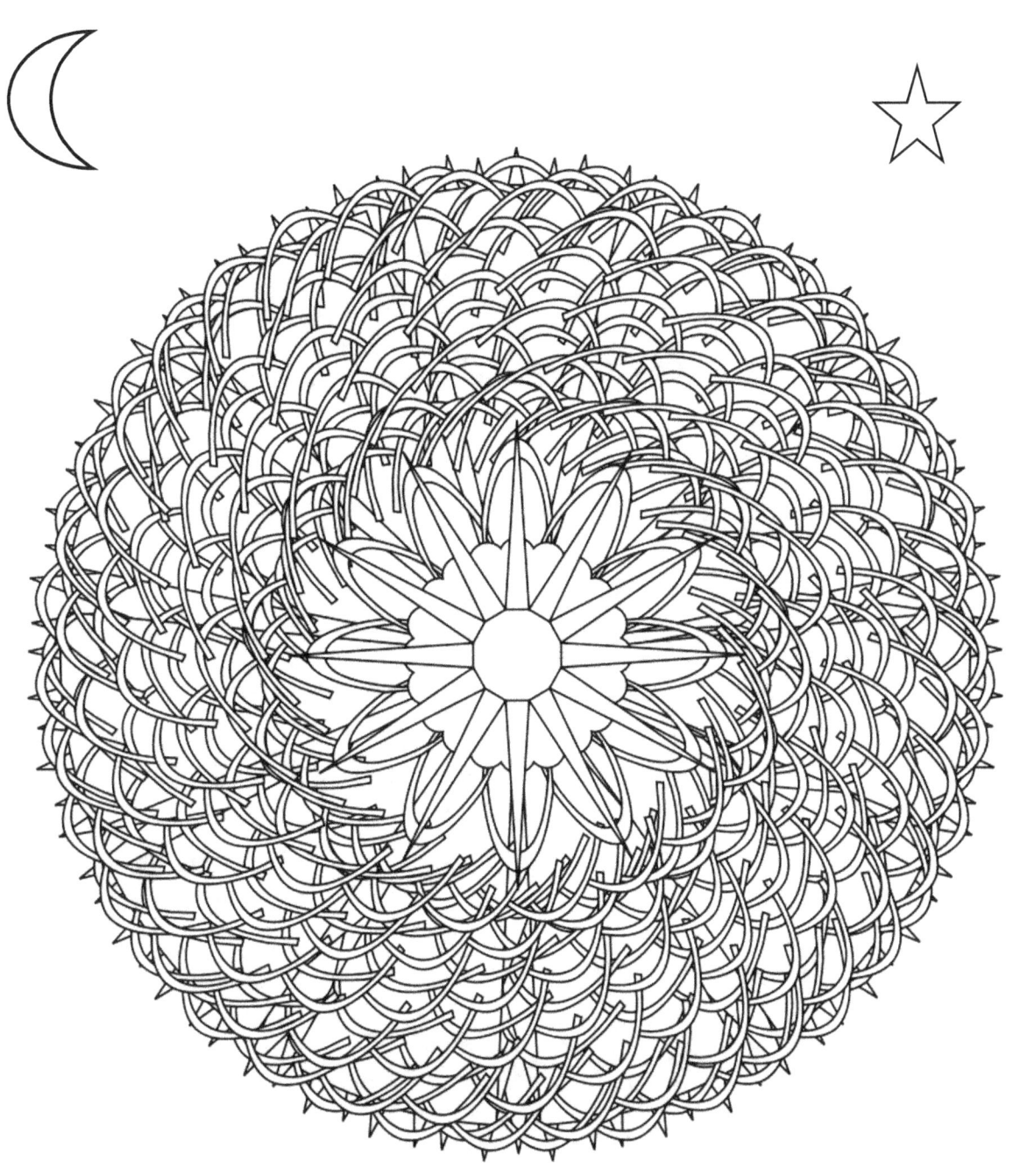

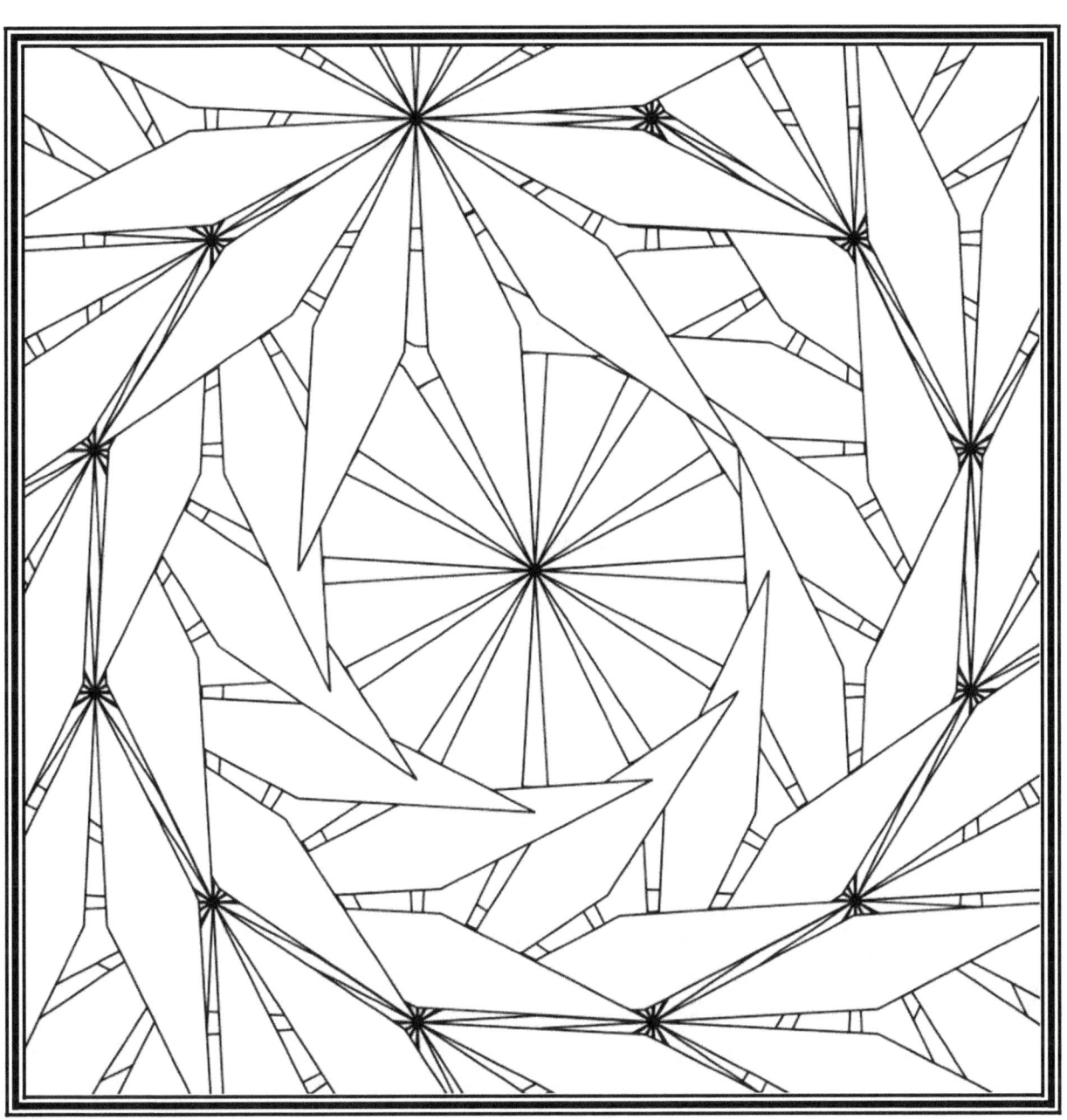

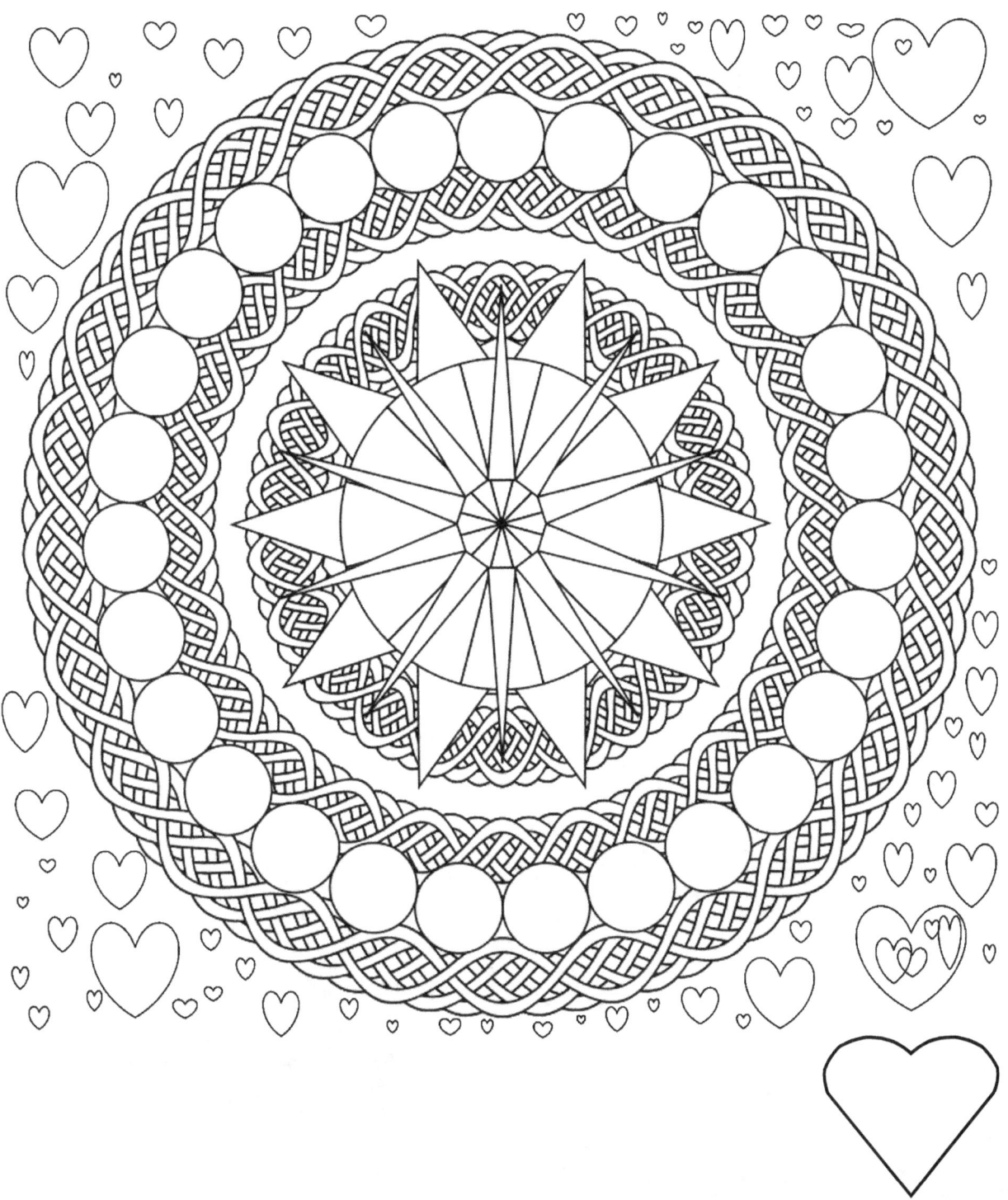

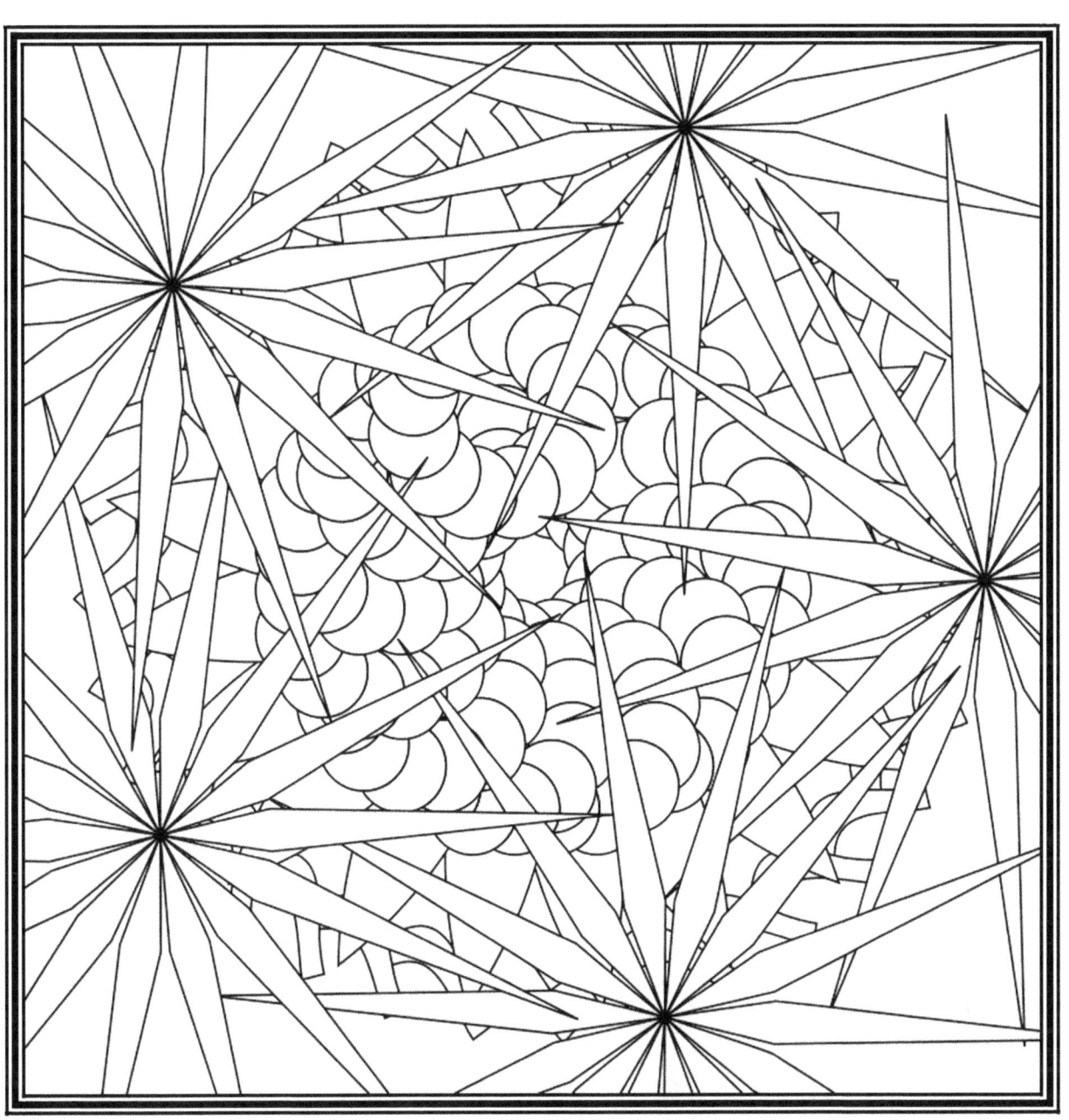

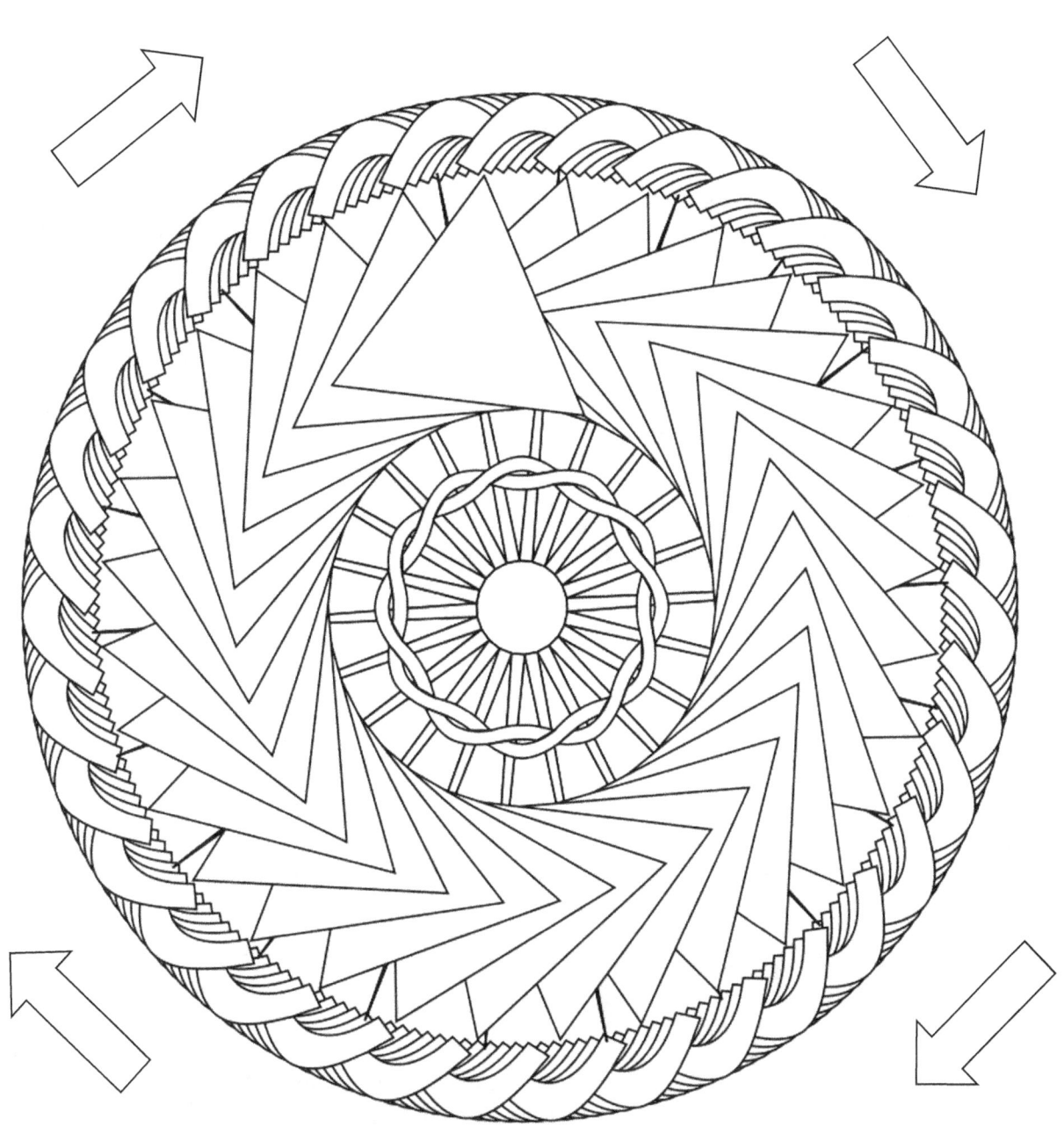

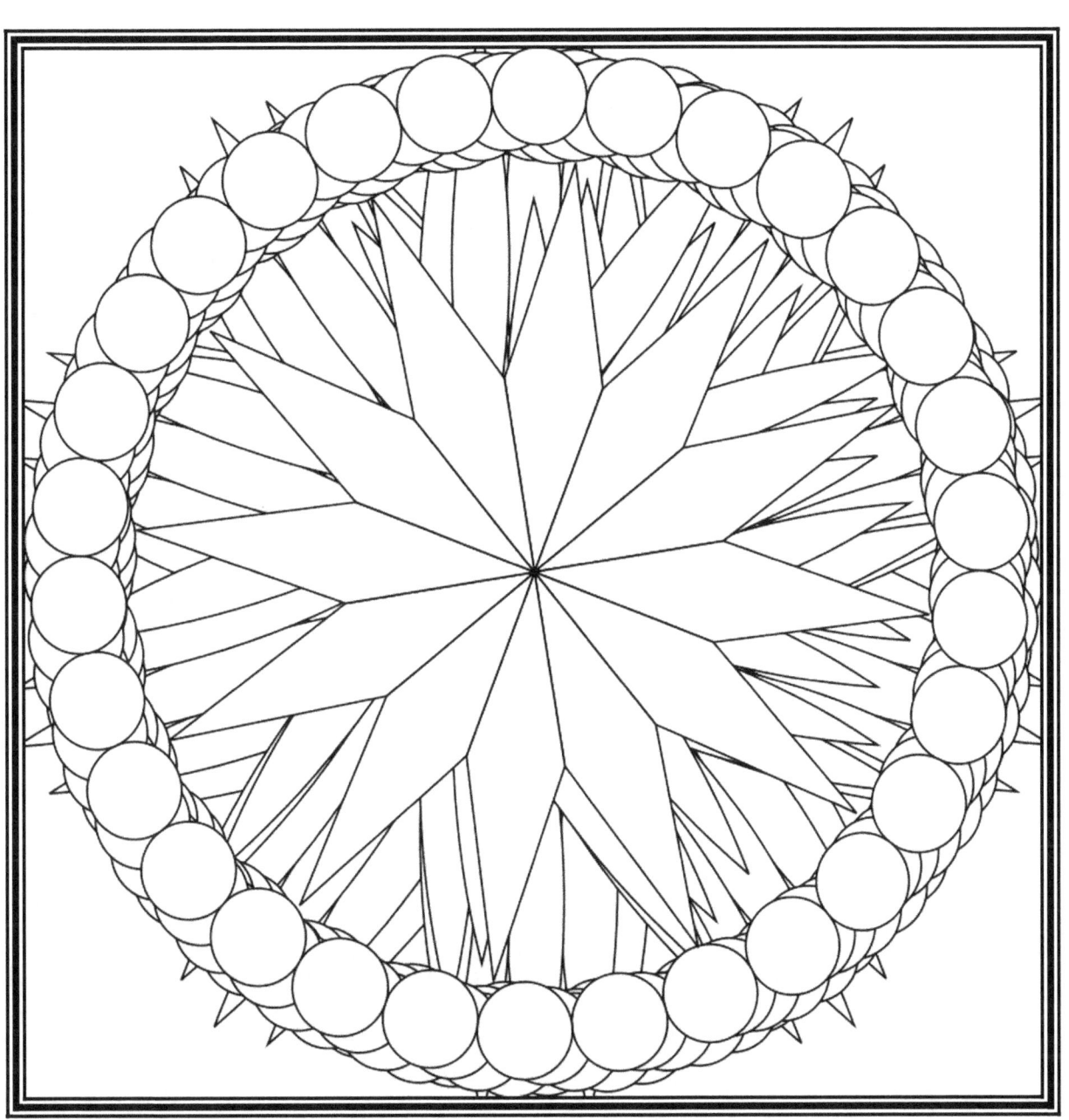

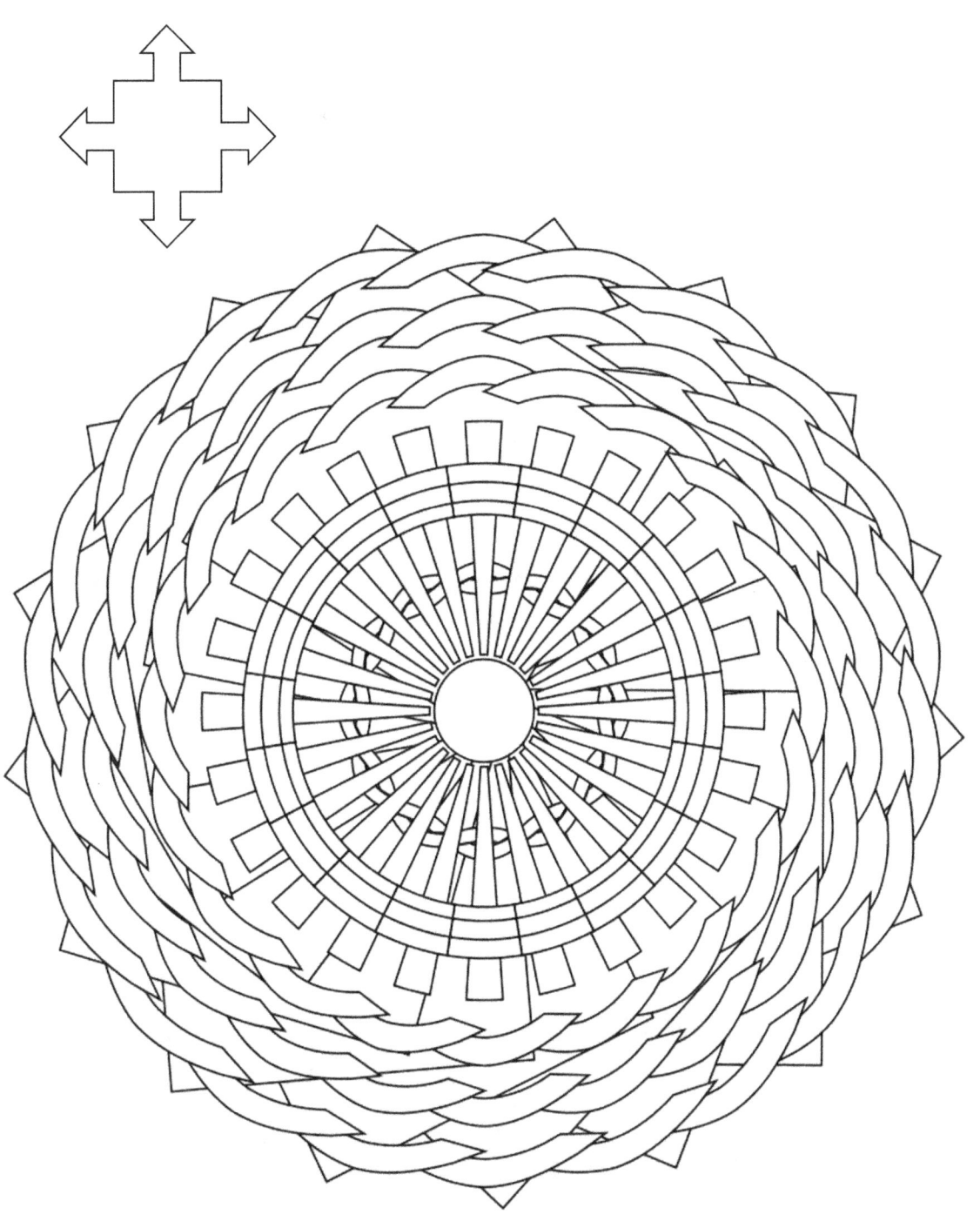

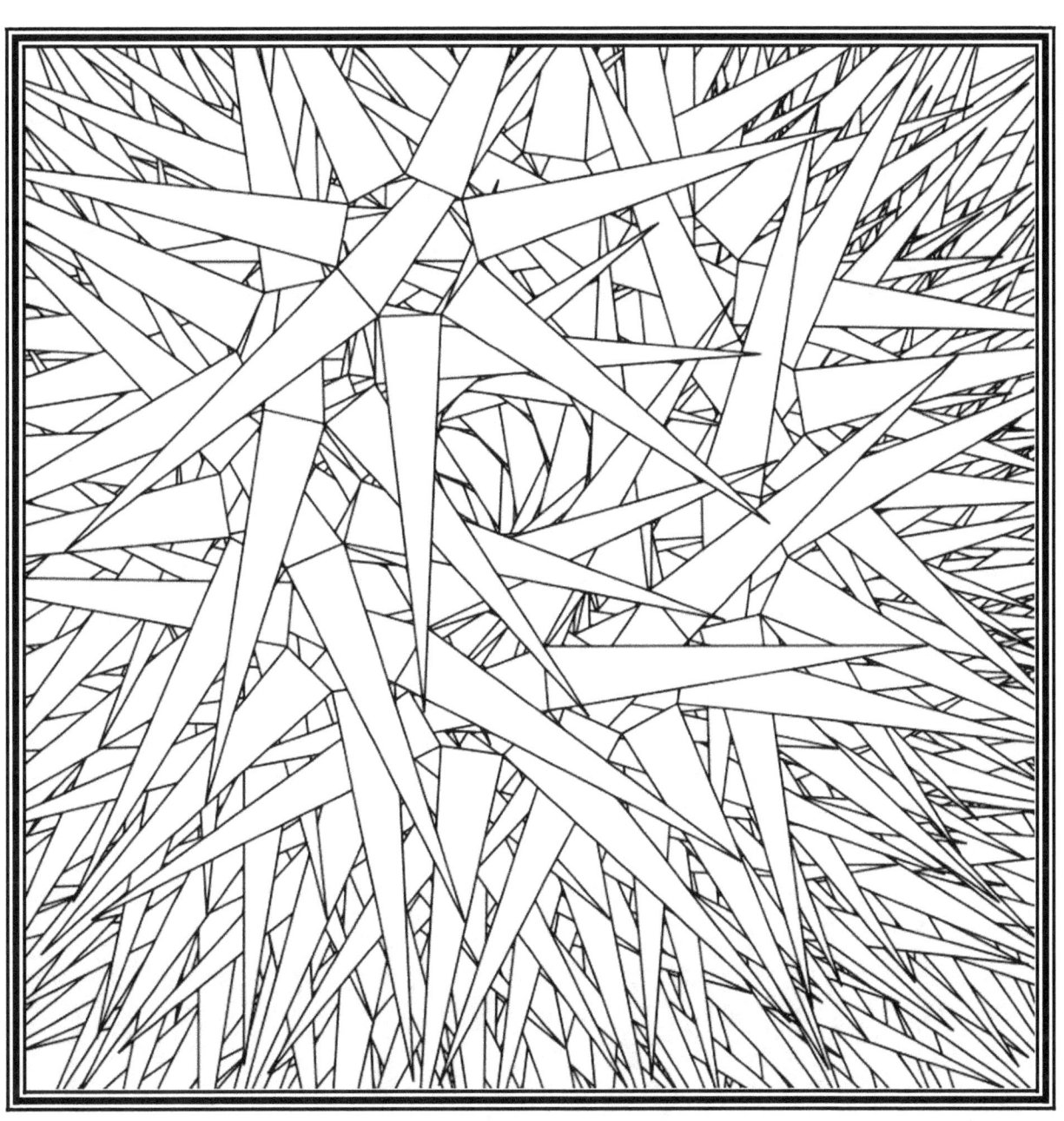

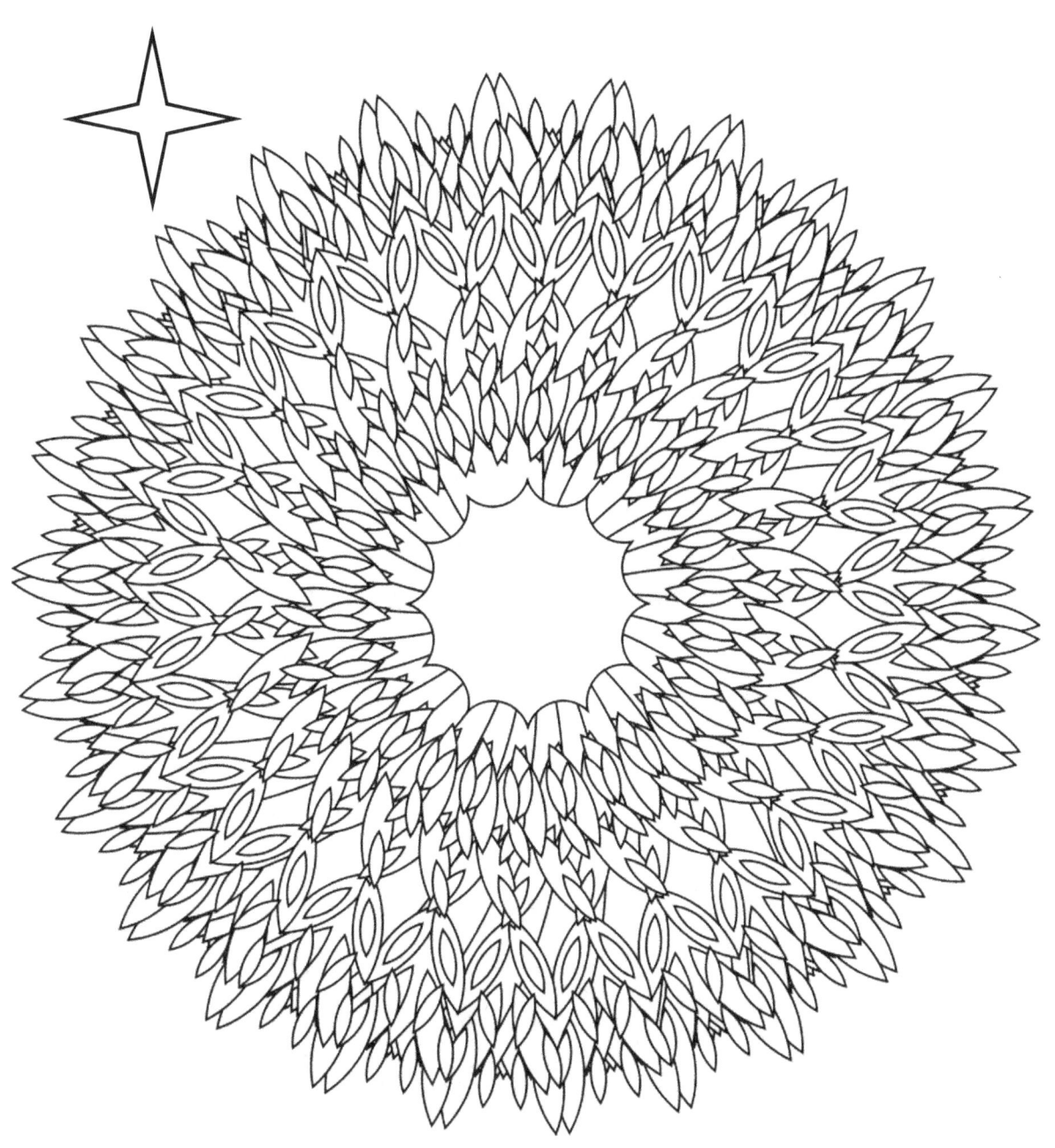

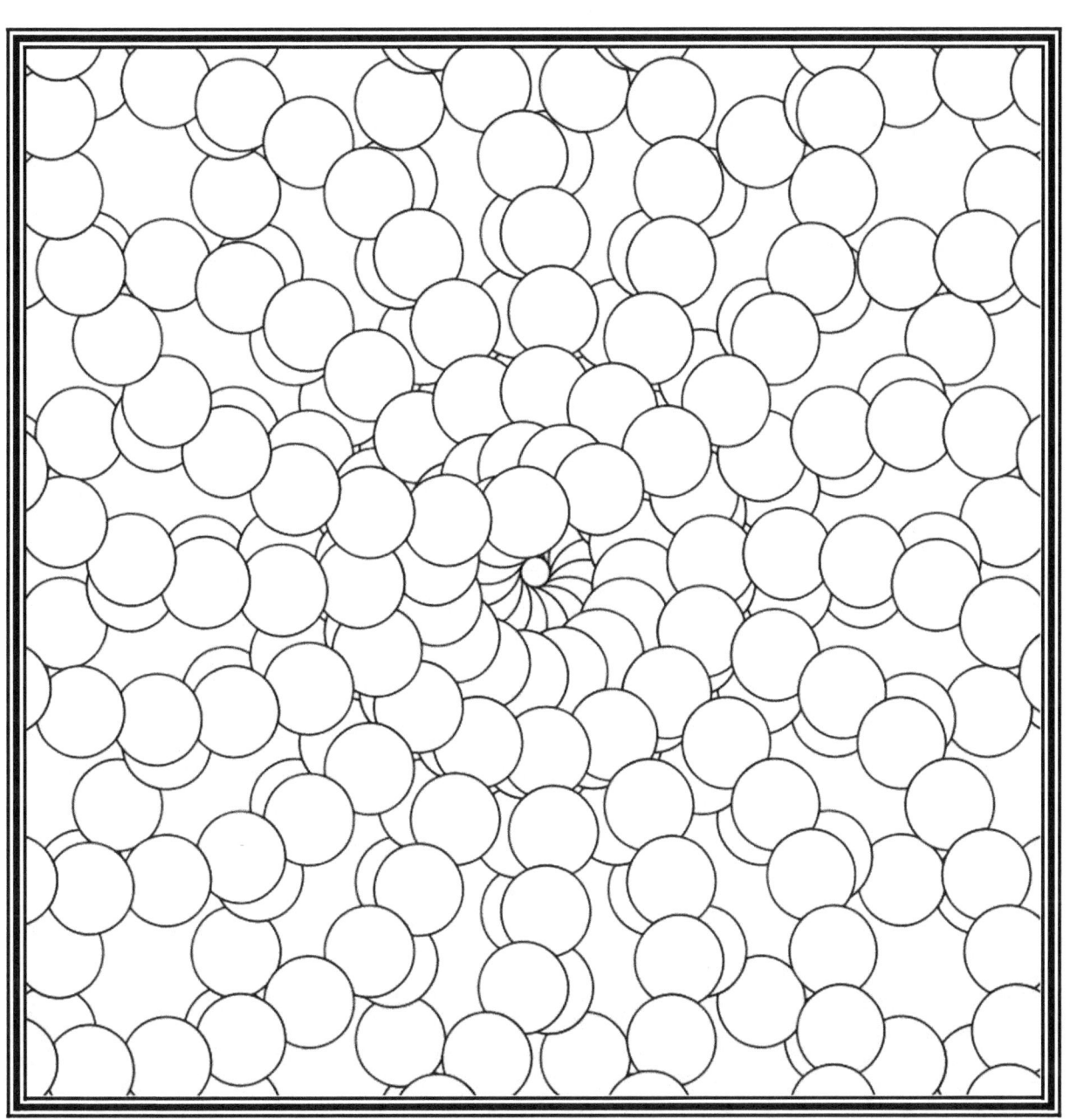

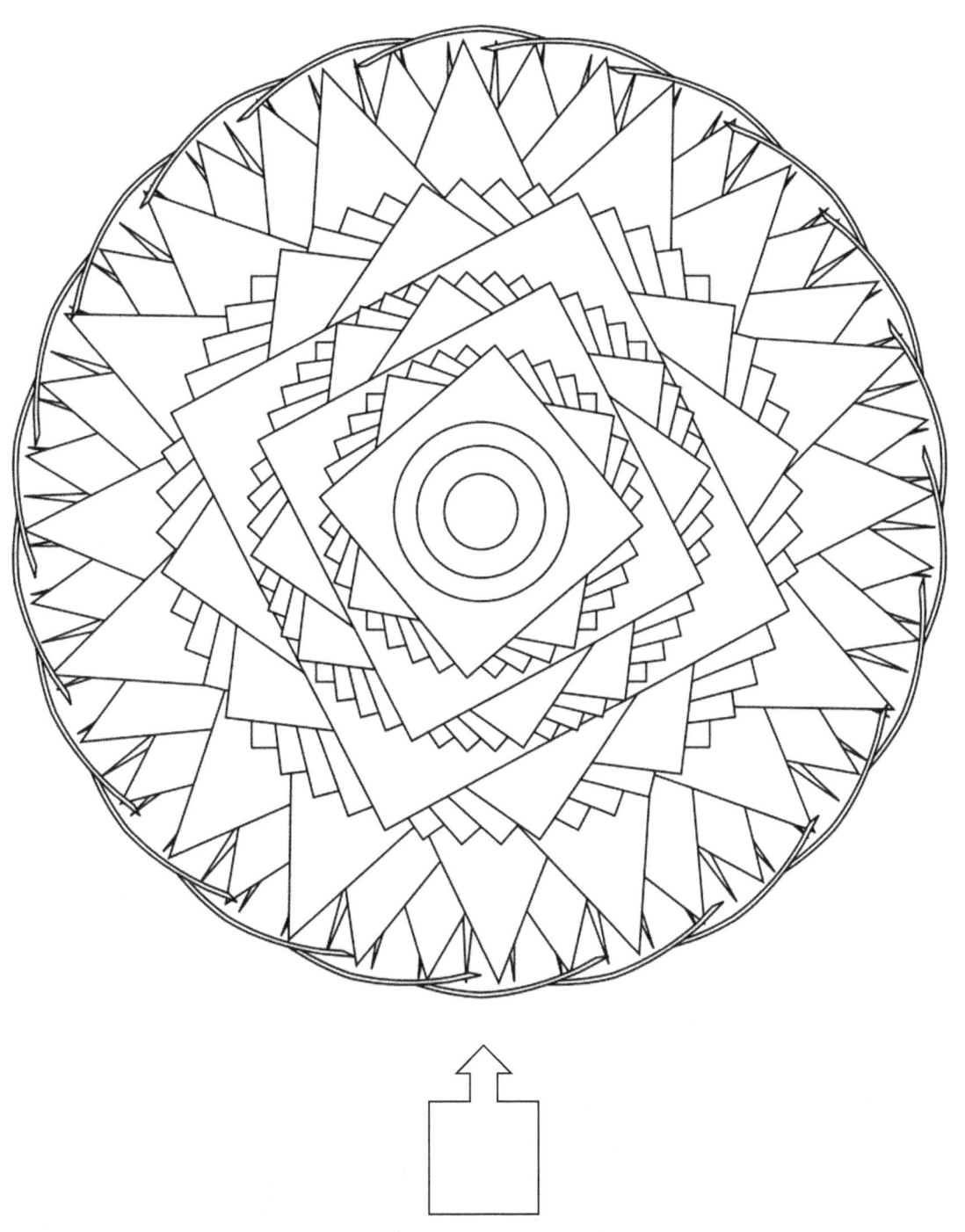

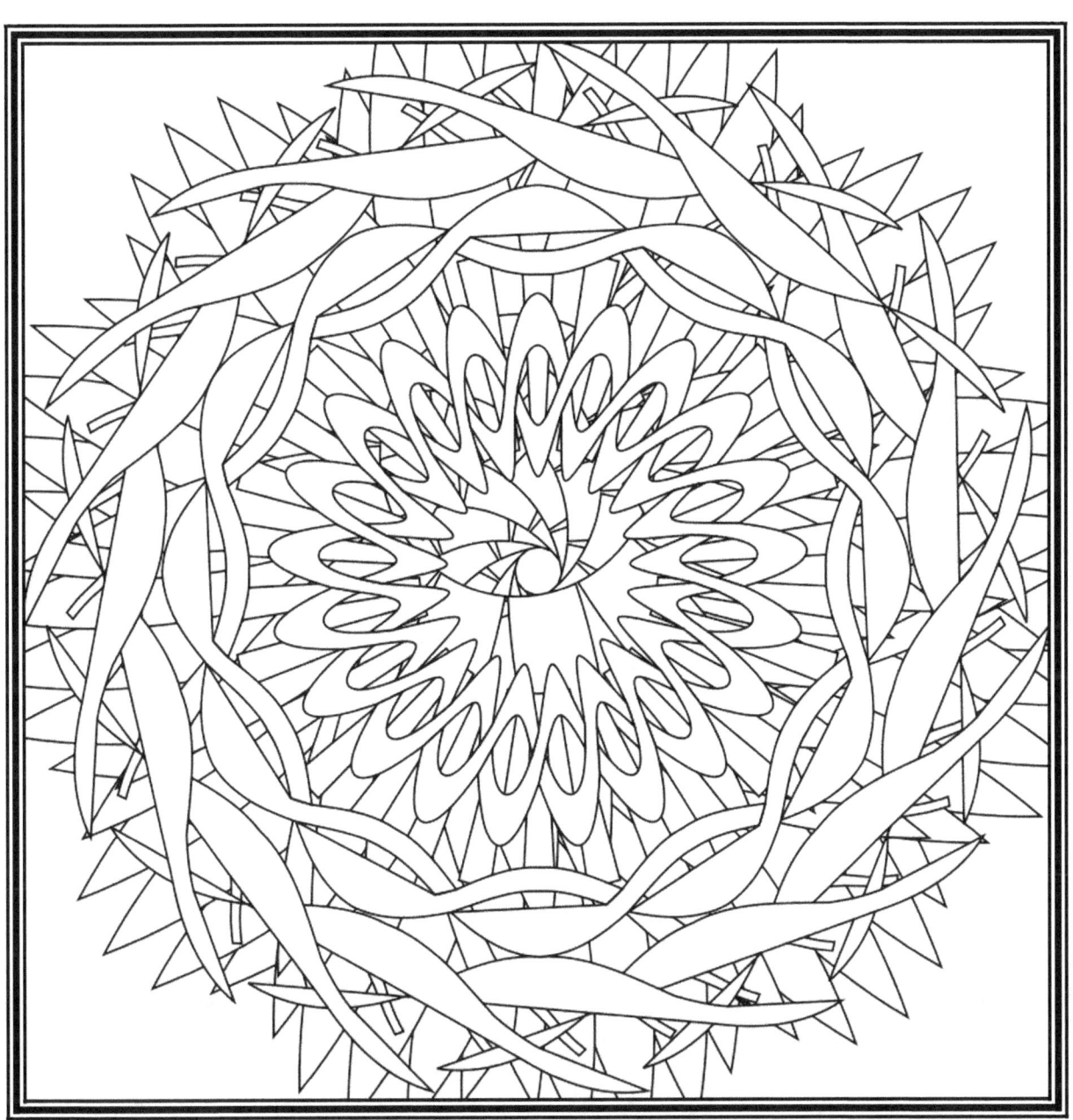

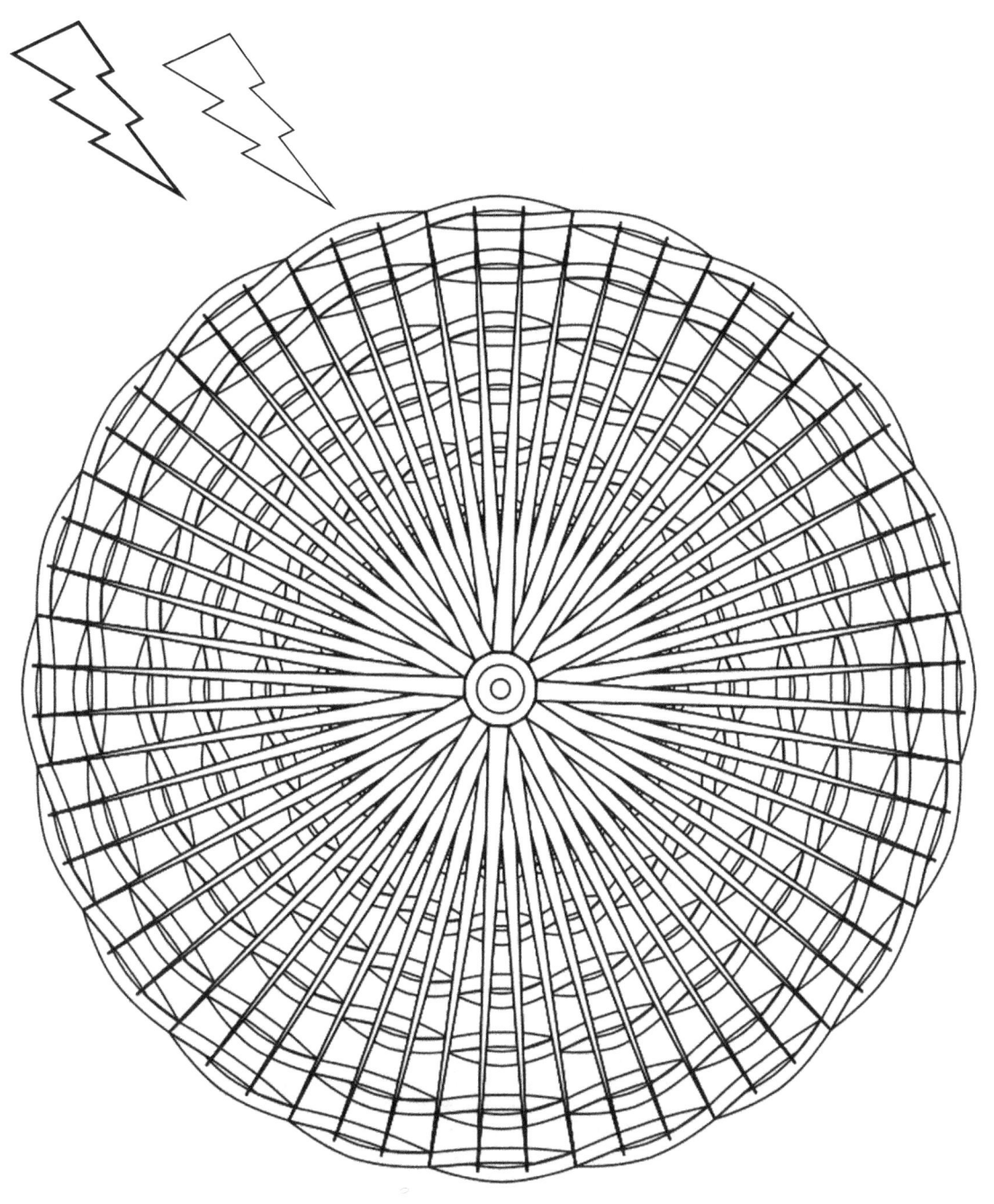

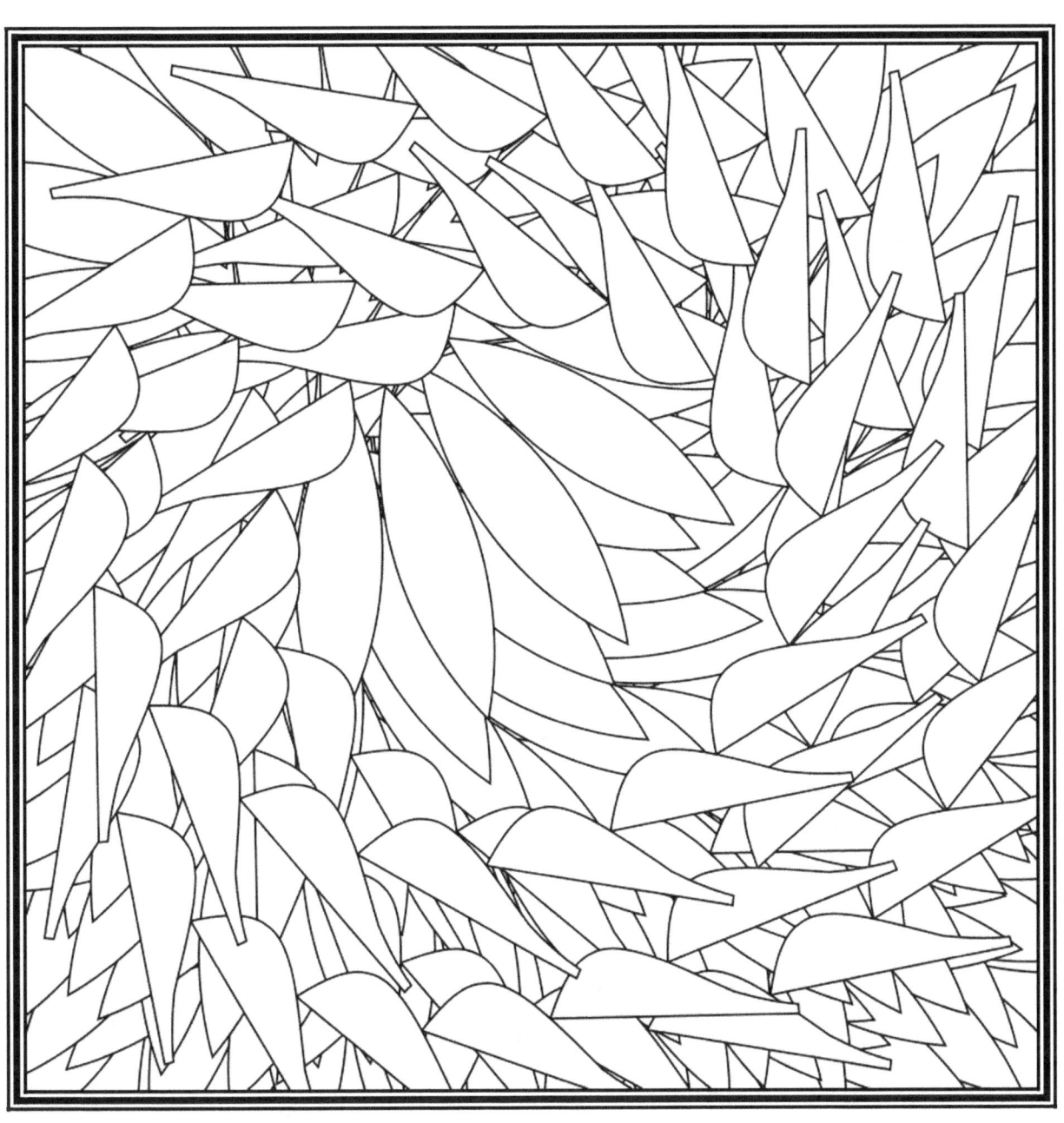

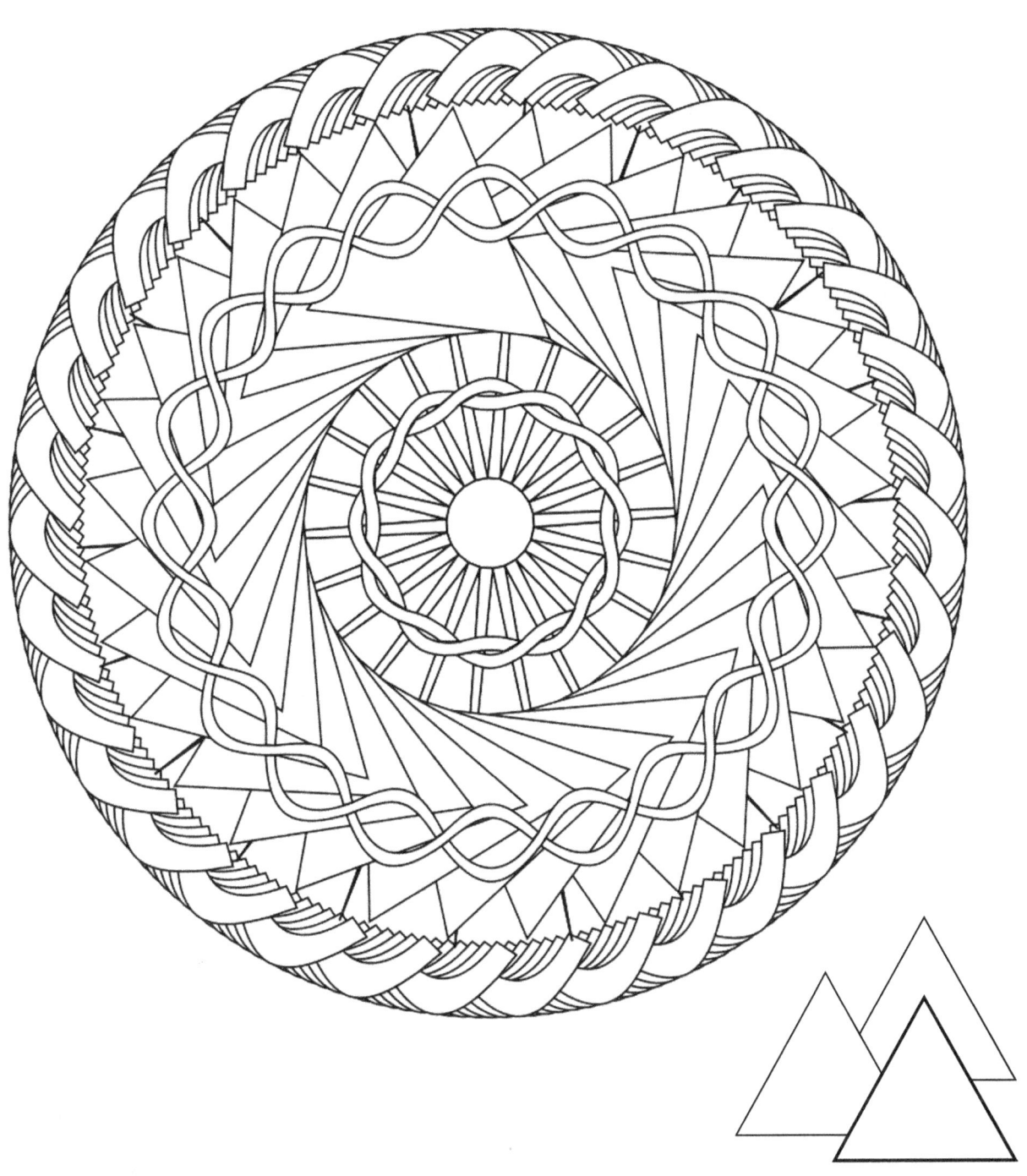

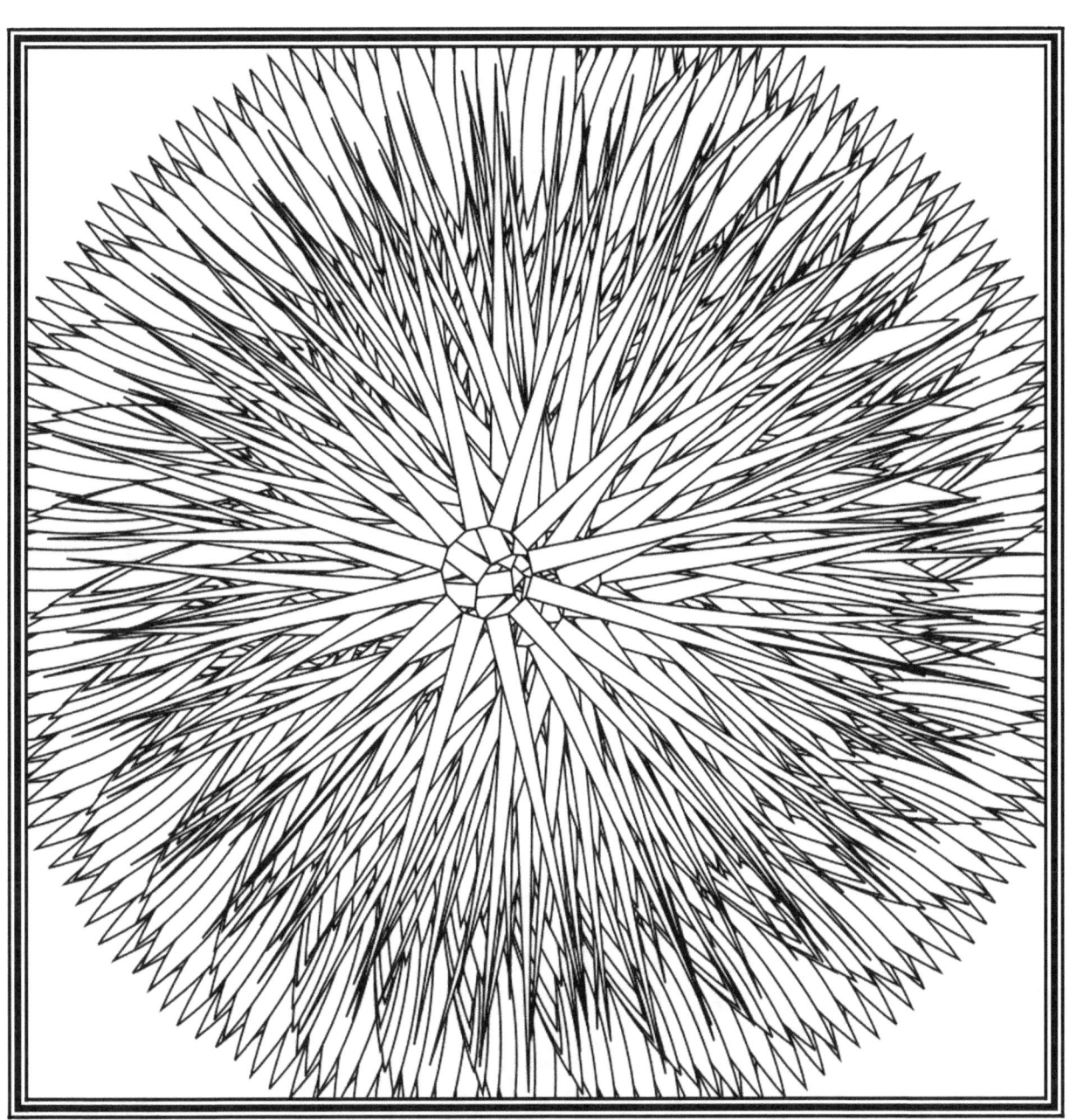

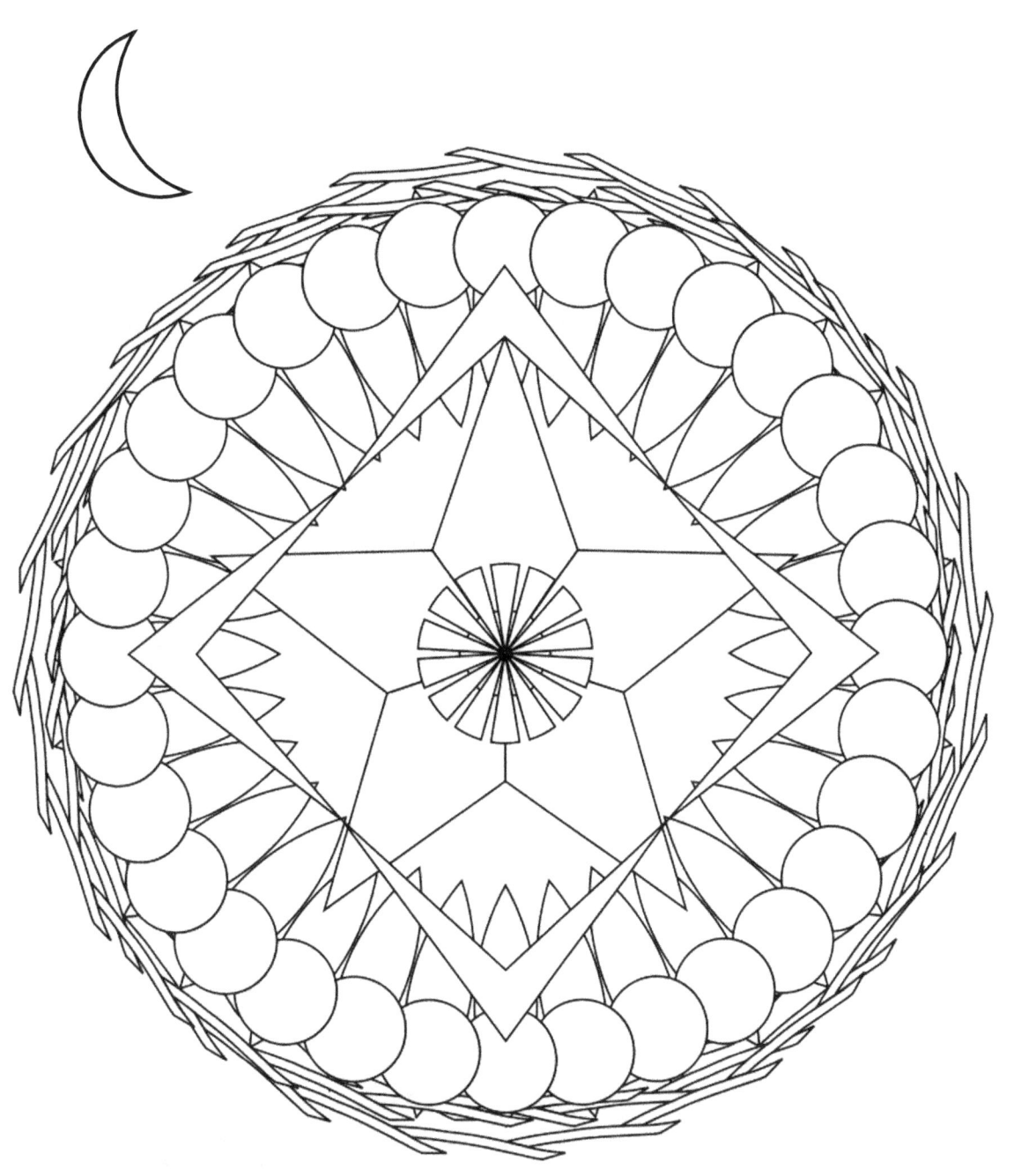

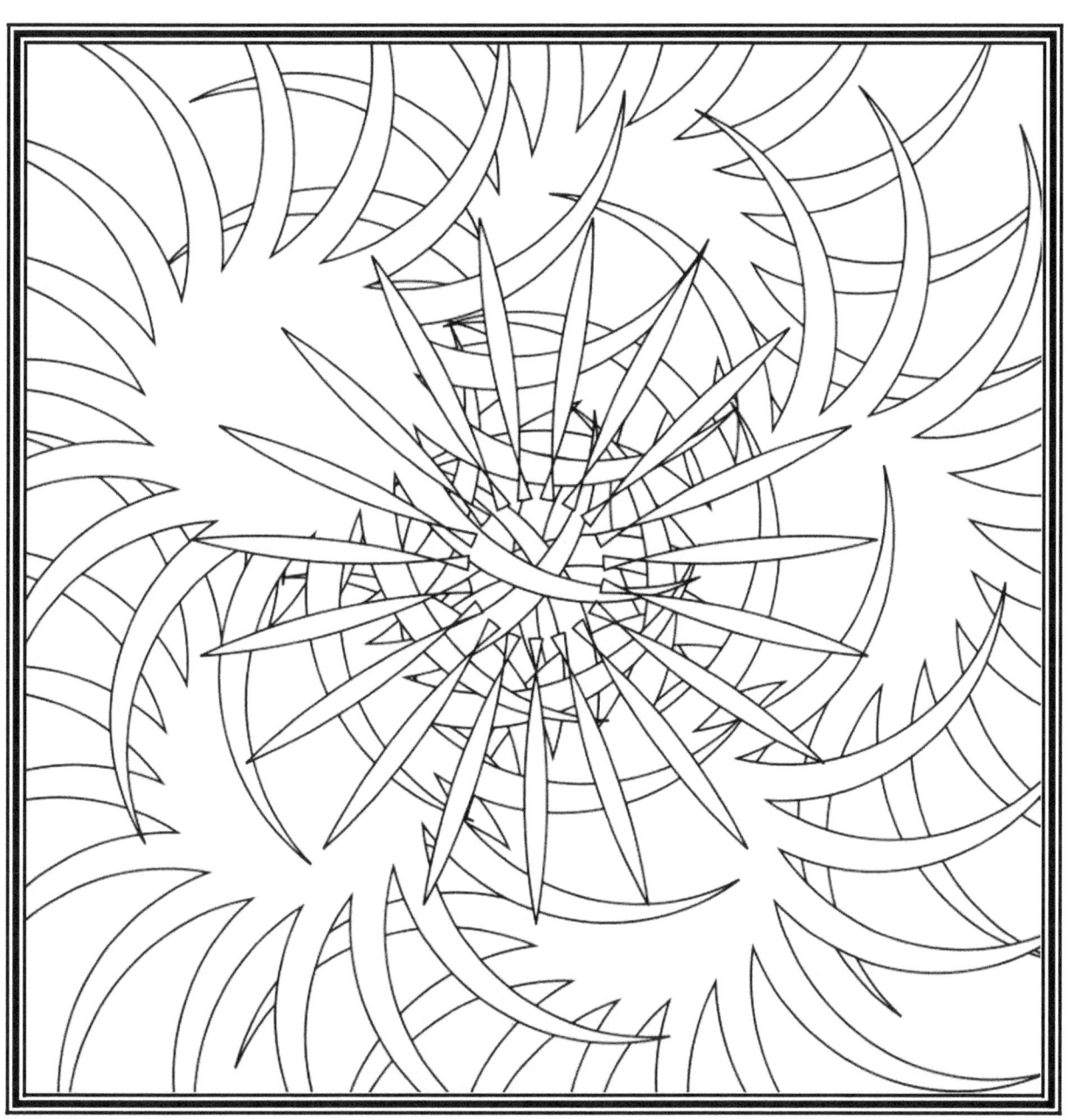

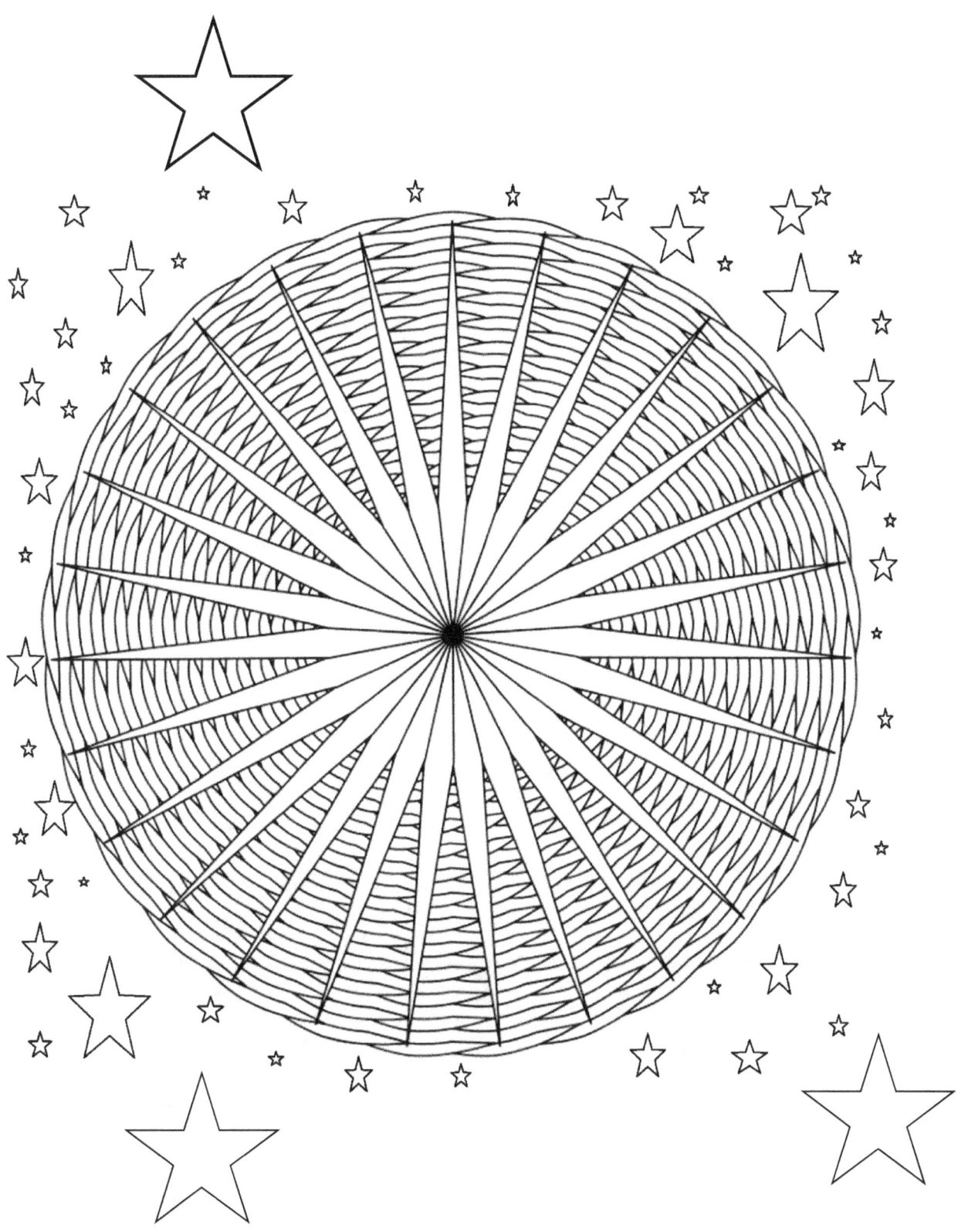

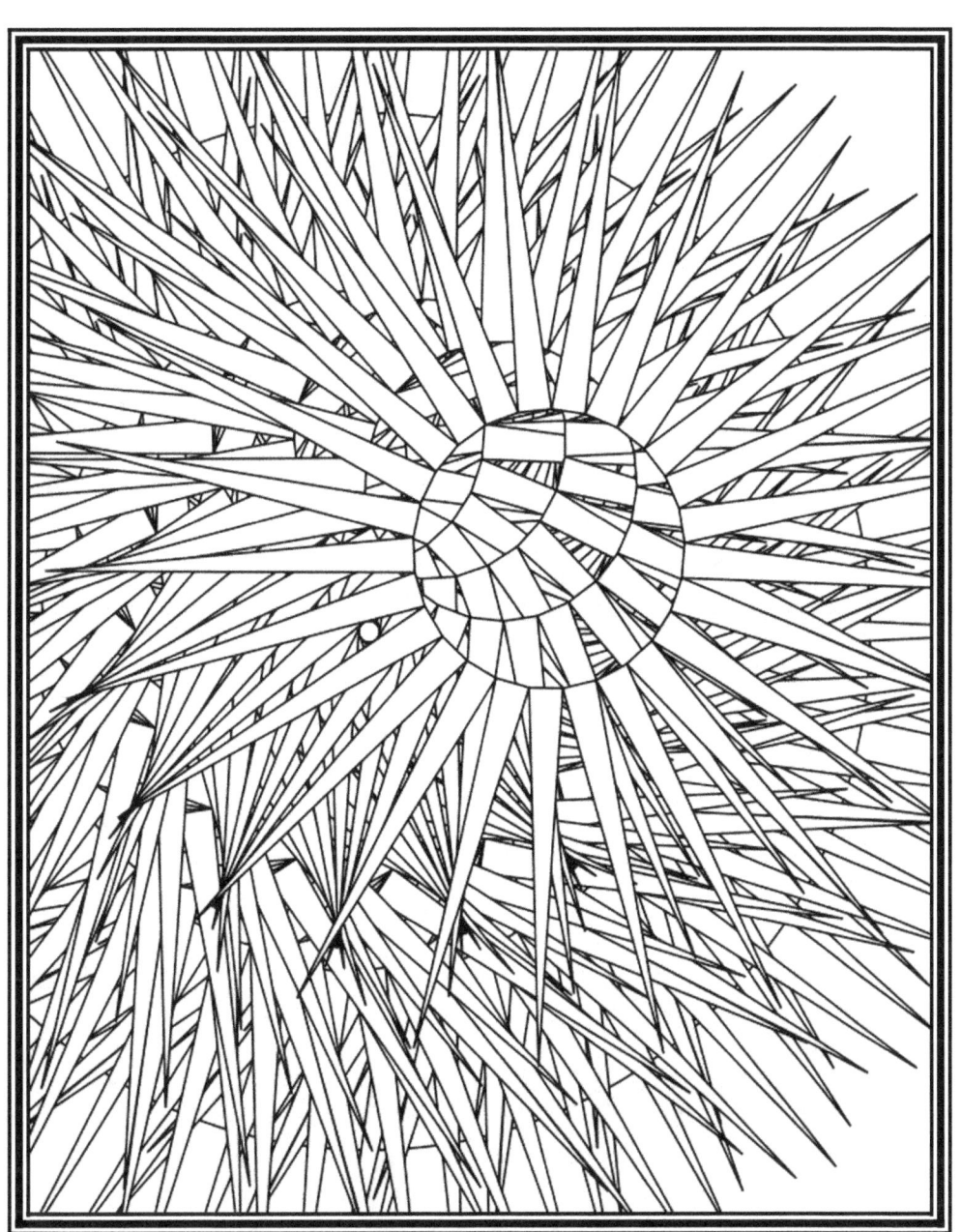

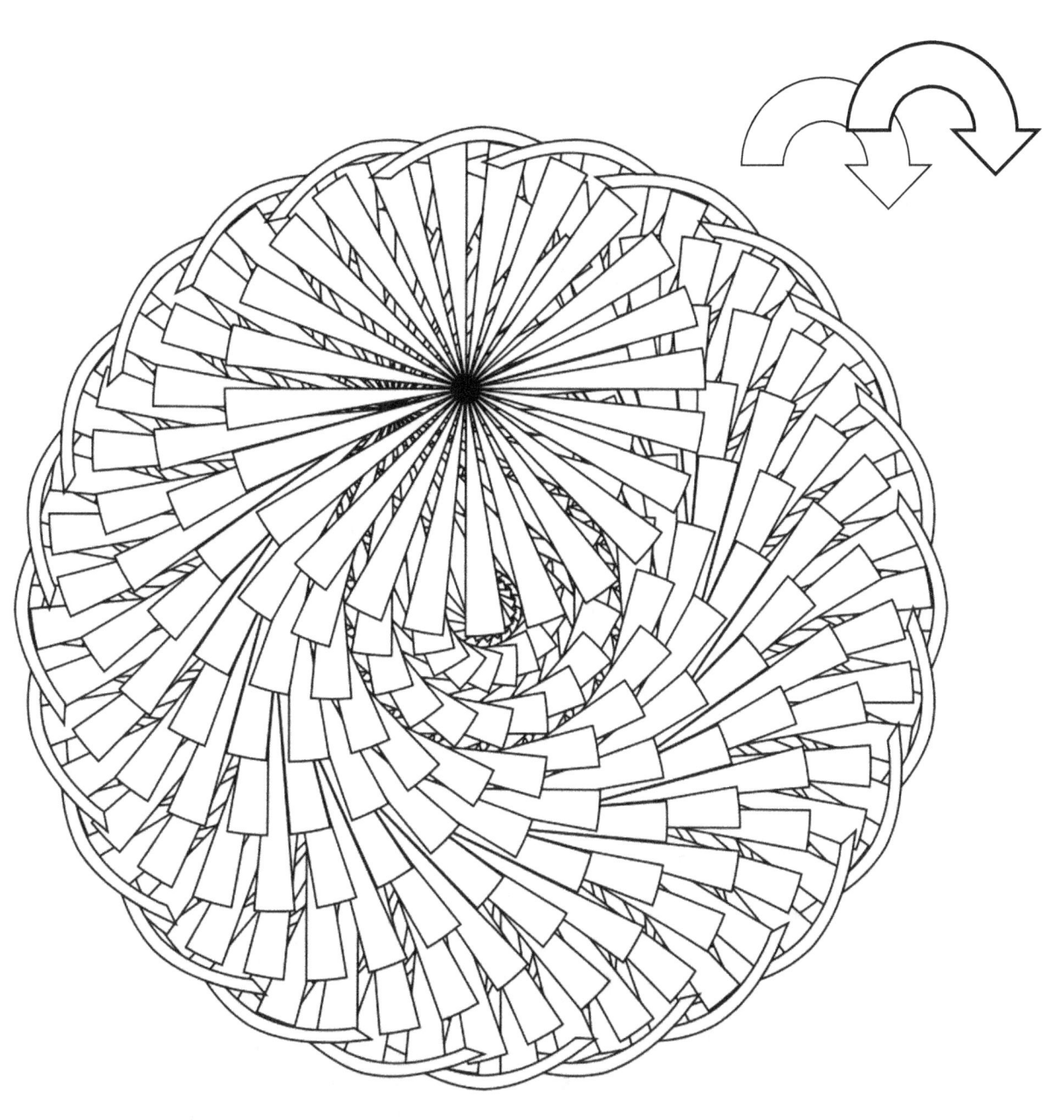

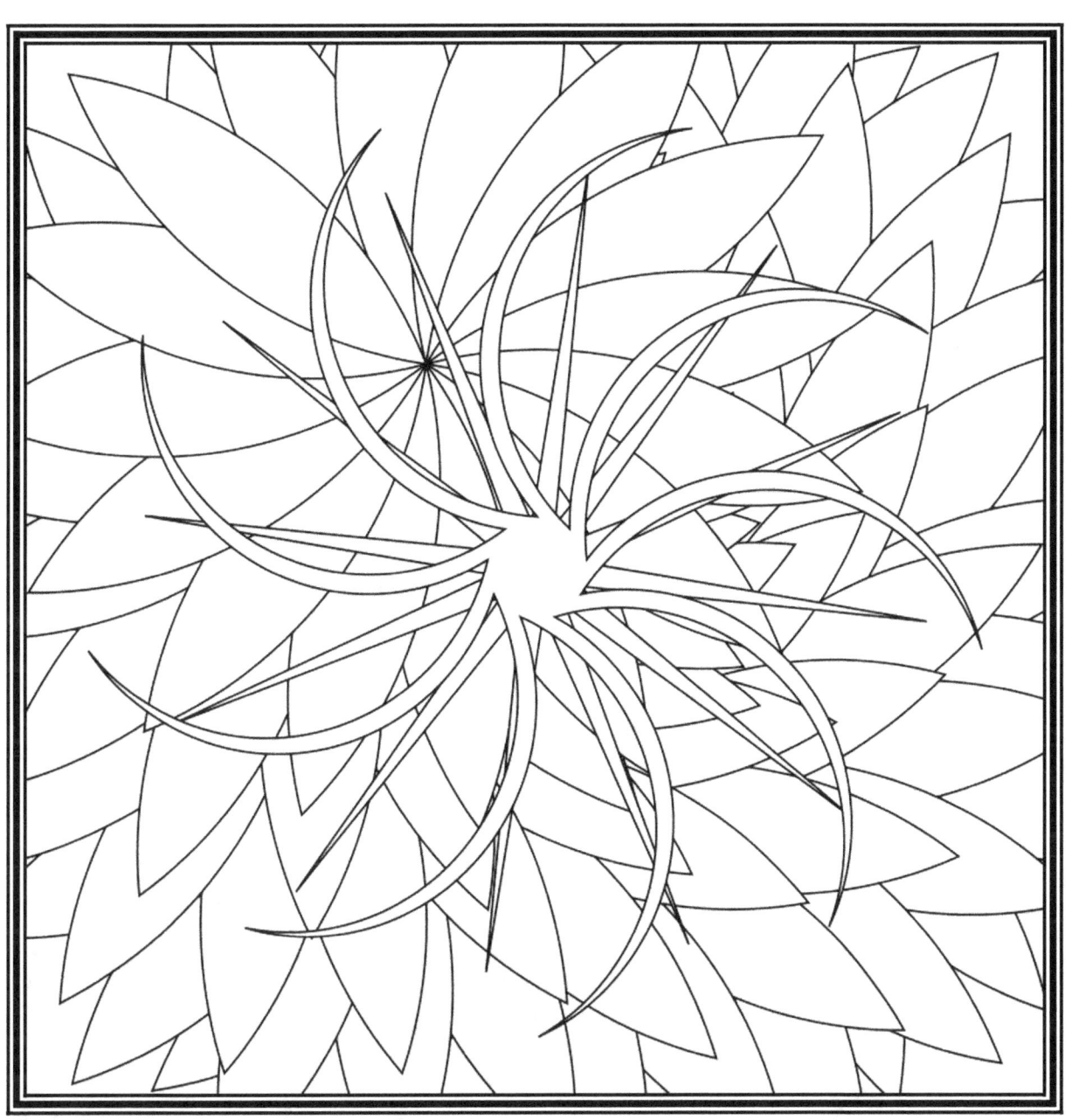

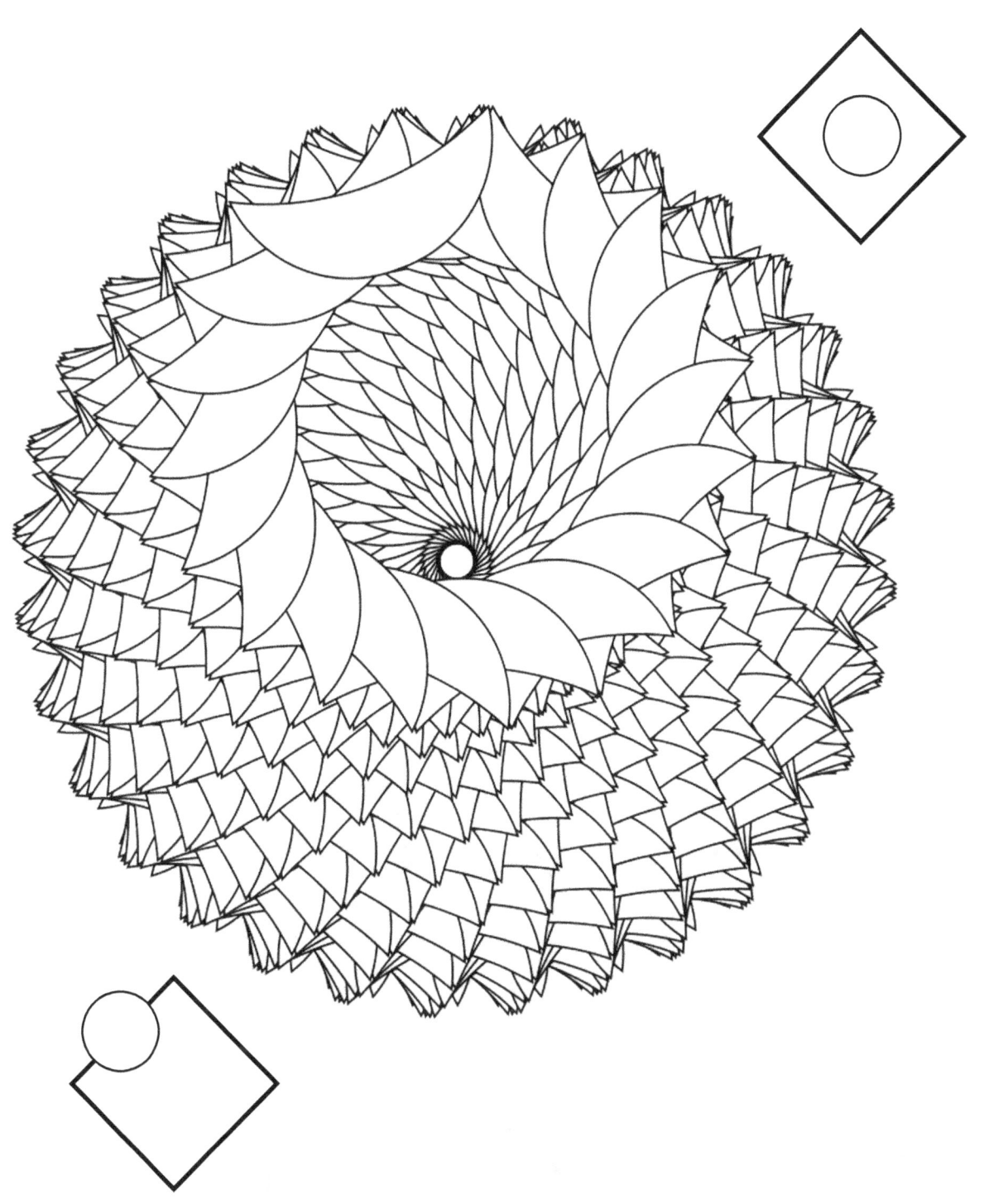

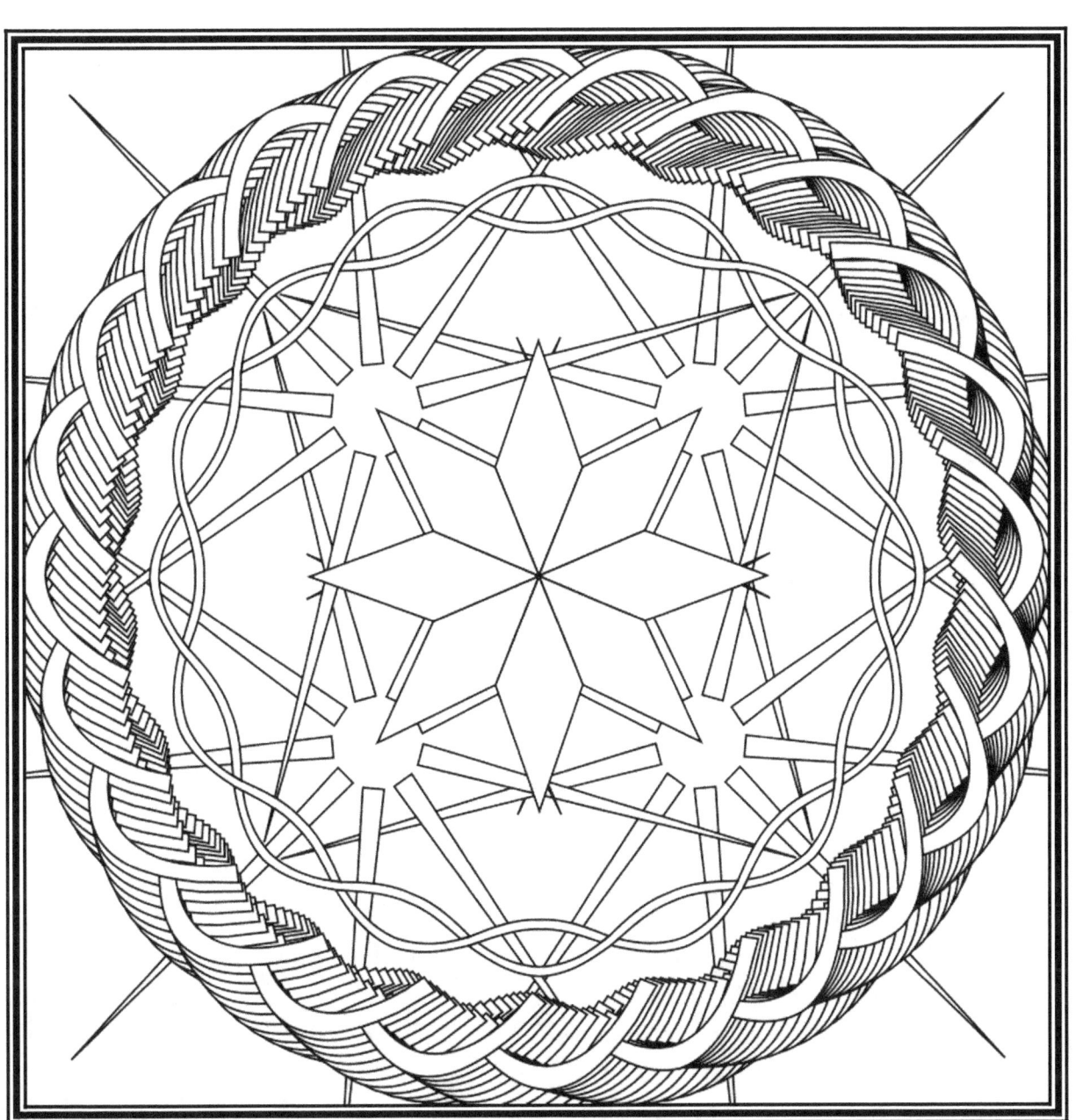

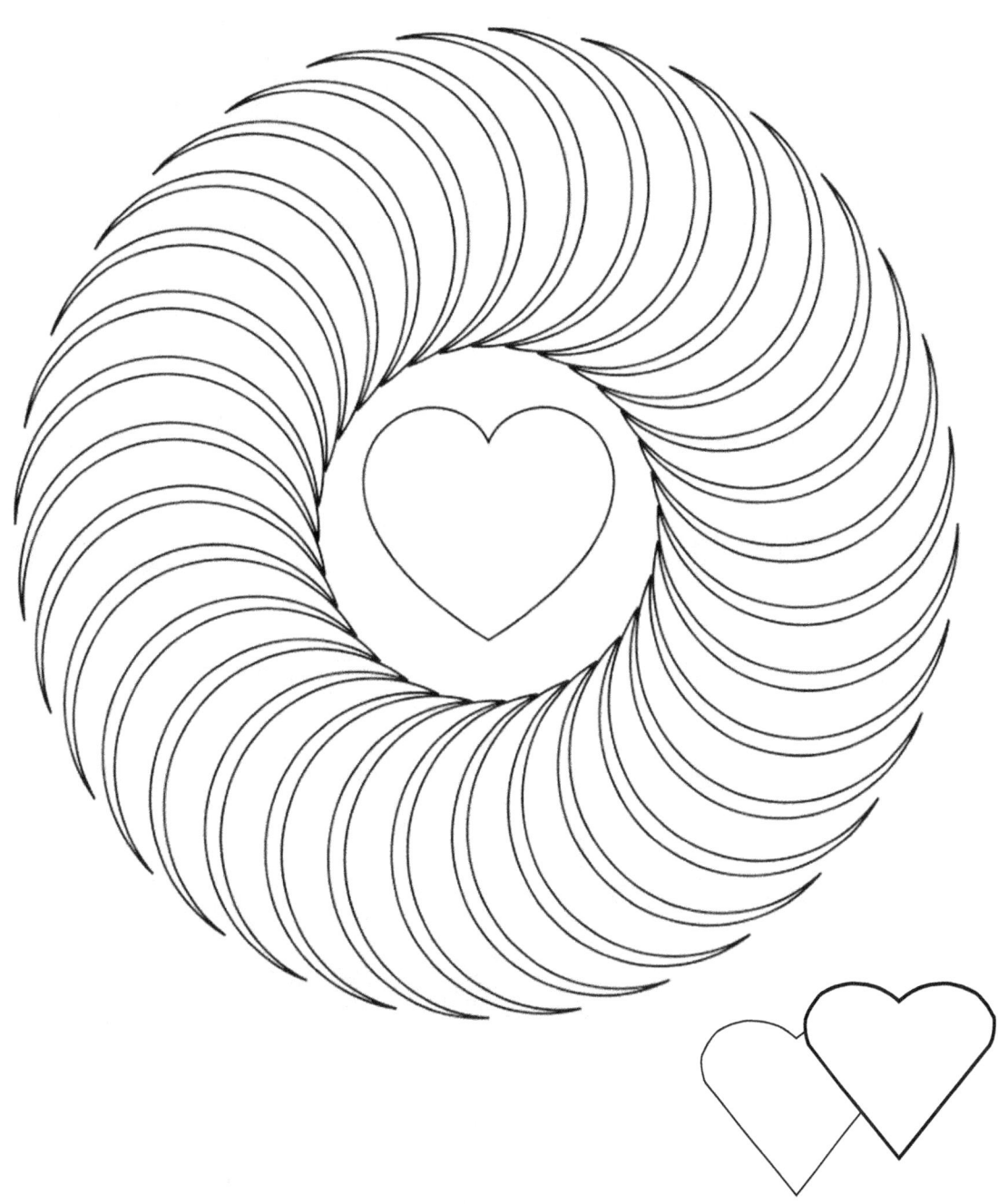

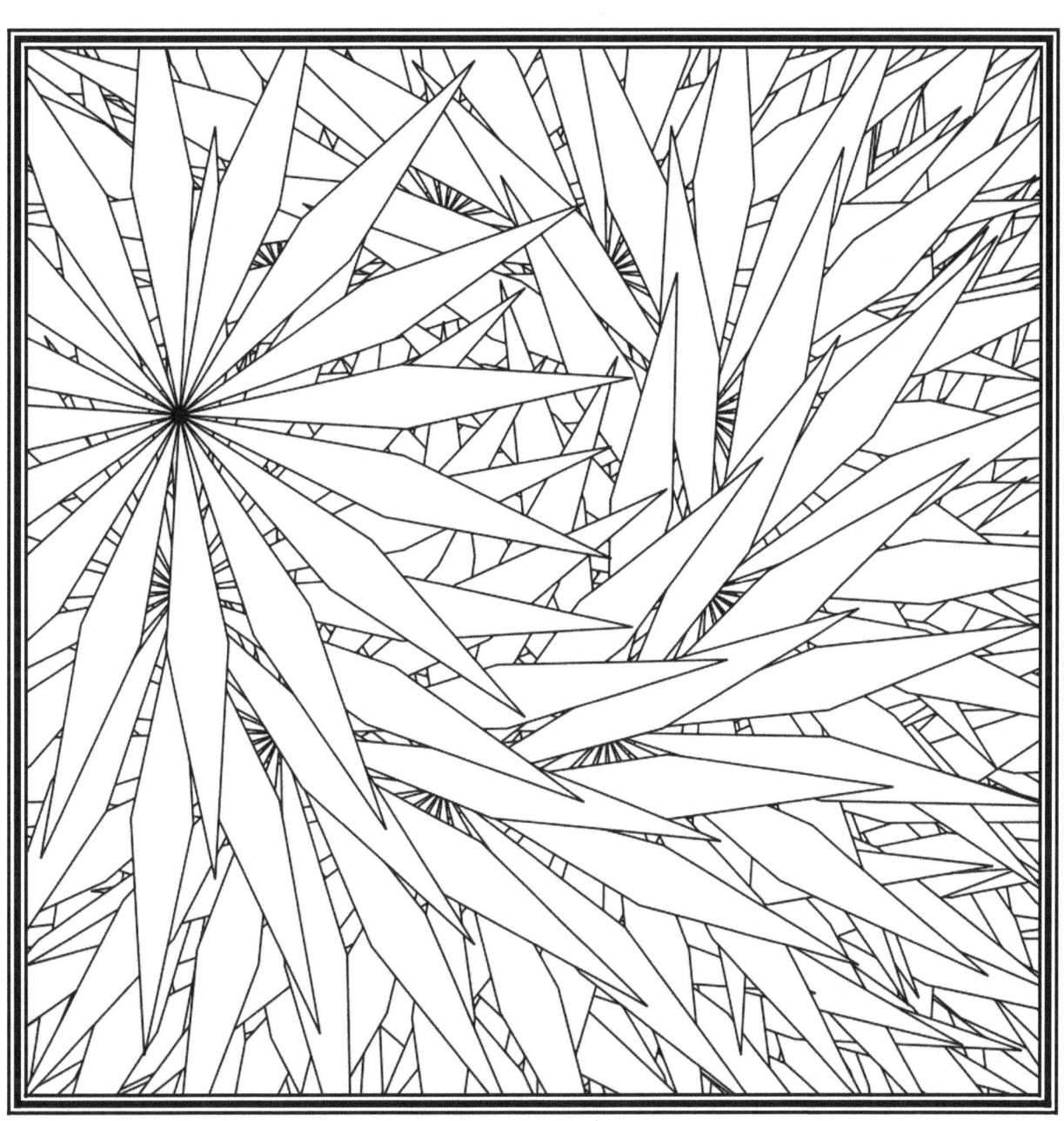

OTHER BOOKS BY D J PARRY

The Gift of Christmas

Siblings Stephen, Thomas, and Amy all grew up loving Christmas…not just the day itself, but all the fun and activities that led up to it. In fact, Stephen loved it so much that he started The Christmas Club, which shared many secret activities aimed at getting people to believe. Then one day, everything changed. Now, years later, Thomas has sworn to never celebrate Christmas again. Then on a snowy Christmas Eve, a large box, filled with a variety of wrapped, numbered packages, and accompanied by a letter from his sister, arrives, putting his resolve to the ultimate test. A heart-warming story that will make you believe in the magic that is Christmas.

How to Start Your Own Lemonade Business

This easy to follow, step-by-step guide for kids contains the basic knowledge needed to start and operate their own lemonade business. From planning the business to choosing a location, from building a stand to making the lemonade, and from advertising to customer service, this manual provides many ideas, tips, and common sense advice for the young entrepreneur. Learning about business has never been so much fun!!!!!